The All-New

Woodworking
for Kids

The All-New

Woodworking
for Kids

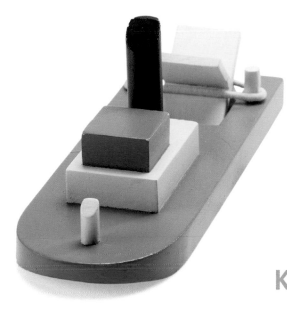

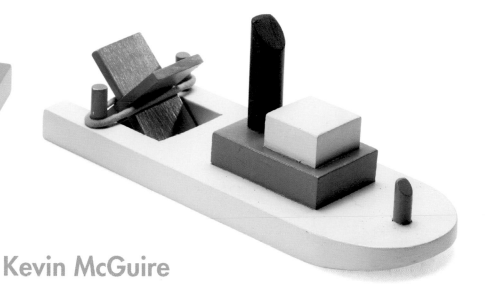

Kevin McGuire

LARK CRAFTS
Asheville

Senior Editor: Wolfgang Hoelscher
Editor: Rain Newcomb
Creative Director: Celia Naranjo
Art Director: Robin Gregory
Designer: Ginger Graziano
Cover Designer: Cindy LaBreacht
Photographer: Steve Mann

LARK CRAFTS

An Imprint of Sterling Publishing
387 Park Avenue South
New York, NY 10016

If you have questions or comments about
this book, please visit: larkcrafts.com

Library of Congress Cataloging-in-Publication Data

McGuire, Kevin, 1952-
  The all-new woodworking for kids / Kevin McGuire.
       p. cm.
  Includes index.
  ISBN-13: 978-1-60059-035-1 (pb-trade pbk. : alk. paper)
  ISBN-10: 1-60059-035-7 (pb-trade pbk. : alk. paper)
  1. Woodwork–Juvenile literature. I. Title.
  TT185.M3797 2008
  684'.08–dc22

                                                    2007049053

10 9 8 7 6 5 4 3

Published by Lark Crafts
An Imprint of Sterling Publishing Co., Inc.
387 Park Avenue South, New York, NY 10016

Text © 2008, Kevin McGuire
Photography and Illustrations © 2008, Lark Crafts, an Imprint of
Sterling Publishing Co., Inc., unless otherwise specified

Distributed in Canada by Sterling Publishing,
c/o Canadian Manda Group, 165 Dufferin Street
Toronto, Ontario, Canada M6K 3H6

Distributed in the United Kingdom by GMC Distribution Services,
Castle Place, 166 High Street, Lewes, East Sussex, England BN7 1XU

Distributed in Australia by Capricorn Link (Australia) Pty Ltd.,
P.O. Box 704, Windsor, NSW 2756 Australia

Manufactured in China

ISBN 13: 978-1-60059-035-1

For information about custom editions, special sales, and premium and corporate
purchases, please contact Sterling Special Sales Department at 800-805-5489
or specialsales@sterlingpub.com.

Requests for information about desk and examination copies available to college and
university professors must be submitted to academic@larkbooks.com. Our complete
policy can be found at www.larkcrafts.com.

Contents

Page 114

Page 132

Page 29

Page 71

Page 60

Anyone Can Build with Wood

You don't need a workshop full of fancy power tools to start building fun and useful woodworking projects. All you need are some wood, some nails, a few simple tools, and this book!

Think of how impressed your family and friends will be when your woodworking projects start making their lives easier. If your dad loses his keys sometimes, he'll flip for a cool key rack. (See page 117.) Does your dog need a comfy place to sleep when she's outside? Give her a fancy new home with the Pooch Palace on page 46. A Study Partner is just the thing your sister needs to help her get her homework done. (See page 103.) Do you want your brother to keep his hands off your CDs and DVDs? Make a spinning media tower so you can store them in your room. (See page 120.)

These are just a few ideas to get you started. There are dozens more in *The All-New Woodworking for Kids.* Many of these projects can be created in an afternoon or two. The first step to making any practical, fun, good-looking woodworking project is to read the next chapter. Have fun!

Woodworking Basics

Supplies & Tools

You don't need a shed that's stocked floor to ceiling with wood or a workshop full of the most expensive tools. Each project in this book begins with a Shopping List and a Tools List, so you'll know what you need to make that project. Just start small and buy the supplies, tools, and wood you need for a single project.

LUMBER

Lumber is the term used to describe wood—usually lots of it. But even if you're buying just one foot-long board for a project, it's called lumber. You can find lumber at your local lumberyard or home-improve-

ment store. **Standard lumber** (the most commonly used boards) is sorted by type, grade, and size.

The **grain** of the wood (the thin, wavy lines that run along it) flows along the faces and edges of the board, and stops at the ends. Knowing the terms for these parts will help you understand how a project fits together.

Types of Lumber

There are two basic types of wood, **softwoods** and **hardwoods**. Pine, spruce, and fir trees are common sources of softwoods. Softwoods are light-colored, lightweight, and fairly strong. It's easy to hammer a nail into a softwood board. One drawback of softwoods is that sometimes they don't have a pretty

Hardwood

Softwood

grain. So they're best to use for projects that you want to paint. (You'll read more about finishing on page 23.) Because softwoods are easy to work with, most of the projects in this book use softwoods. Unless a project tells you otherwise, use softwoods.

Poplar and oak trees are common sources of hardwoods. Hardwoods are generally heavier and more durable than softwoods. They can cost more, too. Because hardwoods tend to have a pretty grain, use them for projects that you want to finish with a **stain** or **varnish**. If a project will look or work best using hardwood, the instructions will say so.

The Parts of a Board
Woodworkers refer to three different parts of a board: **edges**, **faces**, and **ends**. The edges are the two narrow sides that run the length of the board. The faces are the board's two wide, flat surfaces. And the two ends are located—where else?—at the opposite ends of the board.

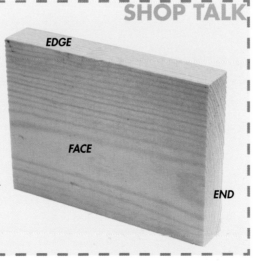

EDGE

FACE

END

Grades of Lumber

Lumber's **grade** refers to how the board looks. So the grade of your lumber depends on how many **knots** and other defects it has. (A knot is the place where a tree's limb entered the trunk of the tree.) The grade can also affect how easy it is to work with the wood—it's hard to hammer or drill into a knot! Unfortunately, better grades cost more. Just buy the best grade you can afford. Clear grade is the best. Select grade is in the middle. (Each board will have one good side and one so-so side.) Common grade has the most knots and defects.

Clear grade

Select grade

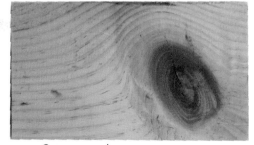

Common grade

Lumber Size

The wood at the lumberyard is sorted, named, and sold by its **nominal** size. Nominal means "in name only." The wood is a slightly different size than its name suggests. The nominal sizes were used many years ago, when the common lumber sizes were thicker and wider. The projects in this book list the nominal size in the Shopping Lists because that's how lumber is sold. For example, if the project tells you to get a 2 x 4, you'll get a

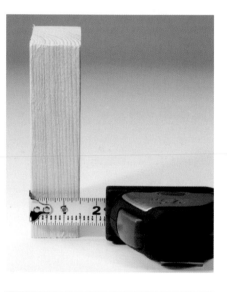

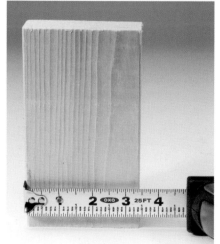

board that's actually 1½ inches high and 3½ inches wide.

Plywood, Dowels, Lattice, and More

Occasionally you'll use wood that comes in a different form, such as **plywood**, which is made from wood slices glued together to form a flat sheet. Plywood is inexpensive yet very strong. You'll use it for large projects, including the workbench on page 36. Like board lumber, it comes in different grades and sizes. The lumberyard will cut plywood to the size you need, so you don't have to wrestle with a huge sheet. (They may charge you a small fee for this service.)

There are a few other special forms of lumber you'll use for these projects: **dowels** (round poles); **lattice** (thin strips); **craft lumber** (small sanded pieces); and **balsa wood** (lightweight, very breakable). You can choose the diameter, thickness, and/or length you want. Lumberyards, home-improvement stores, and some craft stores sell these items.

Cut List

Each project includes a handy chart like the one on the next page. It tells you everything you need to know about the wood you'll use for

TIP

When you're ready to buy lumber for a project, take this book and your tape measure with you to the store. If you need help, show the project's Shopping List to a salesperson.

CUT LIST

Code	Part	Number	Size	Material
A	Leg	4	1½" x 3½" x 29¼"	Softwood
B	Leg brace	4	1½" x 3½" x 21"	Softwood
C	Top	1	¾" x 2' x 4'	Plywood

Scraps   SHOP TALK

What is scrap wood, exactly? Every time you cut a piece of lumber to the size it needs to be, you have a leftover piece of wood. This is scrap wood—save it! Put the scraps in a scrap bin. Use them to build other projects and to protect your workbench when you drill and finish your project.

the project. If you want to know what the pieces you cut are called, what types of wood they should be, and how many you need, just look at the chart. The chart also tells you the actual dimensions each piece should be after you cut it.

OTHER SUPPLIES

The supplies listed here will get you off to a great start. You'll add more supplies as you make more projects. When you choose a project to make, remember to check its Shopping and Tool lists. You may need to add to the list before you begin the project.

- Finishing nails: 1¼ inch (3d), 1½ inch (4d), and 2 inch (6d)
- Common nails: 2½ inch (8d) and 3¼ inch (12d)
- Brads: No. 17 x ¾ inch and No. 17 x ½ inch

- Phillips flathead wood screws: sizes 6, 8, and 10
- Sandpaper: 180-grit and 100-grit
- Wood glue (yellow carpenter's glue)
- Latex primer
- Latex satin or semigloss enamel paint
- Oil-based sanding sealer
- Oil-based stain and varnish
- Mineral spirits
- Paintbrushes: 2-inches flat, 1-inch flat, and a selection of smaller detail brushes
- Clean, lint-free rags, newspapers, and paper towels
- Sticks for stirring
- Safety glasses
- Paper dust masks

Dust mask

Safety glasses

Paintbrushes

Sandpaper

Wood glue

Latex paint

Electric drill

Bits

Screwdrivers

Hammer

TOOLS

You'll need basic tools to make most of the projects in this book. The pictures show some items that can go in a basic toolkit. Good tools can be expensive, so add tools when you can afford them and when your project requires them. Eventually, you'll have all these tools. (Of course, if someone in your home already has some, save money by sharing tools until you get your own.) You'll find more information about each of these tools in the next chapter.

- Pencil
- Tape measure, 8 or 12 feet long
- Pocket square
- 2 clamps, 6-inch
- Claw hammer, 14- or 16-ounce
- Handsaw*, total length 20 inches or less
- Screwdriver, No. 2 Phillips
- Coping saw (with a selection of replacement blades)
- Rasp (half-round) fitted with a handle

TIP

Always buy the best tools you can afford. Cheap tools aren't any fun to use. They don't work well and they don't last long. For instance, a dull, bent saw won't ever cut straight. And that'll just make it harder to build your project.

- Electric ³⁄₈-inch drill, and a selection of bits.
- Electric jigsaw with a selection of blades
- #12 Extension cord, 25' length

* You can use a crosscut handsaw or a ryoba saw instead. See page 14 for more on saws.

Electric jigsaw

Rasp

Clamps

Coping saw

Crosscut handsaw

Ryoba saw

Square

Tape measure

WORKSHOP SAFETY

Building safely is the only way to go. Why? Because all the fun disappears when someone gets hurt. Think of your tools as friends who treat you just as well as you treat them. Give them the respect they deserve, and they'll do wonderful things for you.

Here are four things to keep in mind while working with wood:

Take Your Time: Don't rush to slap a project together. There's no hurry. When you go too fast, you're more likely to make mistakes. Or worse—injure yourself!

Take Breaks: Try to limit how long you work on a project at any one time. When you start feeling tired or are having trouble concentrating, the best thing to do is walk away for a while, get some fresh air, and relax. When you're ready to start work again, you'll feel much better, and you'll do much better work.

Pay Attention to Your Work: Pay close attention while you work. If you find that your attention is drifting, put everything away and call it a day.

Ask an Adult for Help: It's always a good idea to have an adult helper around while you're working with wood. Two heads are almost always better than one, and four hands can do a lot more than two. An adult helper can assist you with holding projects while you hammer them together or help you with tools you're uncomfortable using.

COMMONSENSE SAFETY

A safe workshop area will help you build your best projects. Whether you set up your shop indoors or out, get some help arranging it so that you have enough room to move boards around and enough light to see your work clearly. Your workbench should be about 30 inches high, sturdy, and large enough to support the tools and lumber that you're using. (The workbench project beginning on page 36 is ideal.)

Pick up any scrap wood off the floor so you don't trip on it, and never leave a board that has sharp nails in it lying on the floor—even for a moment.

If you have long hair, tie it up or wear a cap so that it won't catch in your tools. Like long hair, loose clothing can also catch on sharp tool edges. Roll up your sleeves, and hang your scarf on a peg before you begin.

Flying nails and wood splinters can hurt your eyes, so wear a pair of safety glasses whenever you pick up a hammer or use power equipment. Keep the glasses clean and store them carefully to prevent scratching.

Oil-based stains and varnishes, mineral spirits, and turpentine give off poisonous and flammable fumes, so when the weather's good, do your finishing work outdoors. When you need to work indoors, keep the windows open and turn on a strong fan to provide plenty of fresh air. And no matter where you work, stay away from any source of heat or open flame.

A paper dust-mask will help keep sawdust out of your lungs. Get several when you buy your supplies so you'll have an extra for your adult assistant. Make sure the mask fits snugly over your mouth and nose. The mask may feel uncomfortable at first, but you must wear it whenever you're sanding. Replace the mask when you can see dirt from the sawdust on it.

Of course, every builder expects a small splinter or scrape now and then, so keep a first-aid kit in your shop.

And remember: you can build safely by taking your time, paying attention to your work, and asking for help when you need it.

Techniques

Making your layouts, sawing, drilling, hammering, and sanding—these are the basic skills you'll need to become an expert woodworker. If you already know how to do some of these things, think of this as a refresher.

This section has complete explanations of all the basic woodworking techniques. There are lots of step-by-step photographs to make it easy for you to learn—or relearn—the skills. Read this chapter before you start your first project. Later, when you're working on a project, you can always turn back to these pages to remind you how to use the techniques.

Cutting

Before you make that first cut, there's lots to do, including squaring, measuring, and marking, or using a pattern or illustration to lay out the piece. You may need to clamp the piece. After you make the cut, there will be times when you'll need to transfer layout marks or patterns onto your project pieces. (These marks will help you build the project.) Each of these steps is explained in this section.

SQUARING

To **square** a piece of lumber is to make sure the end of the board is perfectly straight. This is the first step you'll take in every woodwork-

ing project. Without a square end, you can't get an accurate measurement, and that means your project pieces won't fit together.

A **square** is a tool you use to check square. ("Square" is both an action and a thing.) A square is L-shaped and has two parts, a handle and a metal blade. These parts are at a right angle (which is square) to one another. The square's shape is important, because its main job is to help you check and make right angles. The blade is marked with inches and fractions of inches, like a tape measure.

Checking a Board's End for Square

1 Hold the side of the square's handle tightly against one edge of the board and hook the metal blade over the board's end.

2 If the board's end lines up exactly with the blade's edge, and no space shows between them, the board is square. Not square? Keep reading to find out how to make it so.

Squaring a Crooked Board

1 Press the edge of the square's handle tightly against the edge of the board. Lay the metal blade flat across the board's face, at least 1 inch from the crooked end.

2 Use a pencil to draw a line along the blade's edge, from one edge of the board to the other. Saw along this line to remove the crooked end. (See page 15 for more information on sawing.)

Squaring Across a Wide Board

Sometimes you'll need to square across a board that's wider than your square.

1 Square across the board as far as you can with your square and pencil.

2 Flip the square to the board's other edge and line up the blade's edge with the line you've just marked. Use your pencil to complete the line.

3 If there's still a gap between the lines you made, use a straight piece of wood (like the Compass Tool on page 32). Line it up between the squared lines you've made. Use your pencil to mark the line.

MEASURING AND MARKING

How will you know where to cut the lumber to make your project pieces? Don't guess! Just measure and mark. You'll need a tape measure, a pencil, and a square. These are your **layout tools**.

Measuring

Use your tape measure to measure the required distance from the end or edge of the board. (Where you measure from depends on whether you are cutting the board to a certain length or to a certain width. In these how-to photos, we measured to create an 8-inch-long piece.)

1 Slip the tape's hook over the board's end or edge. You'll notice that the hook is a little loose. Don't worry; it should be.

2 Pull the case so the tape extends along or across the board. Make sure the tape is straight—if it's at an angle your measurement will be off.

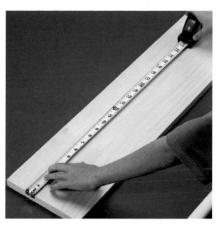

3 Find the length you need on the tape measure and use your pencil to mark that spot on the board.

4 Line up the arm of the square with the spot you marked, just as you did when squaring a crooked board (see page 12). Use a pencil to draw a line along the blade's edge, from one edge of the board to the other.

USING PATTERNS

With some projects, especially ones with curving lines, you'll use a pattern to transfer the shape of the piece onto the board. You'll need to either trace the pattern or photocopy it (and sometimes enlarge it).

Tracing Patterns

1 Set the pattern flat on your work surface, and put a piece of tracing paper on top of it. You'll see the pattern through the tracing paper. Tape the tracing paper in place. Lightly trace the pattern.

2 With scissors, carefully cut out the pattern on the tracing paper.

3 With your wood flat on your workbench, hold or tape the cut-out pattern to the wood's face. Trace carefully around it with your pencil.

USING AN ILLUSTRATION

For some projects, you'll need to make marks on the project pieces to show where the center is, or places where you'll drill holes for dowels or screws. These are referred to as layout marks. Use your tape measure and pencil to transfer the layout marks shown in the project's illustration onto your pieces. See the section on drilling (page 21) for help with the drilling part.

Cutting and Labeling Pieces

Now you're ready to clamp, cut, and label the pieces you need for your project. You'll use a **handsaw** for cutting lumber to length and making **rip** cuts. You'll use a **coping saw** to cut curves or make inside cuts. All these techniques are explained in this section.

CLAMPING

A clamp acts like an extra pair of hands that makes sure your board stays put on the workbench when you saw it. The miter box and bench hook you build on page 26 and page 34 can be used in place of clamps in some instances. Read about how and when to use them on those pages. (When you drill holes in pieces you've cut out, you'll need to clamp the piece to the workbench, as well.)

Using Your Clamp

1 Lay the board on the workbench, with the line you want to cut hanging over the edge of the workbench by about 2 inches. If you're right-handed, clamp the board so the line you want to cut will hang over the right edge of the workbench. If you're a lefty, switch the board to the workbench's left edge.

TIP

Put a small, flat piece of scrap wood between your project pieces and the clamps. This will keep the clamps from denting the project's surface.

2 Now put the clamp in place, with one of the grippers on the board and the other on the workbench. Make sure it won't get in the way of your saw.

3 Turn the clamp's handle clockwise (to the right as you're looking at it). This will tighten the clamp and hold the piece firmly in place.

4 If you're using more than one clamp, position them both loosely (so they hang on) and then slowly tighten them. Tighten one clamp a little bit, and then tighten the other.

5 Make sure the clamp is tightened securely. Now you're ready to cut. Readjust your clamp and your work piece whenever necessary as you continue with your project.

HANDSAW

The saw you'll need is called a crosscut handsaw. It cuts straight lines both across the grain (called **crosscutting**) and in the same direction as the grain (called **ripping**). You can get either a Japanese ryoba saw that cuts on the pull stroke, or a crosscut panel saw with teeth that cut on the push stroke. (See photos of the saws on page 10.) Use whichever kind you prefer. Get a wooden-handled saw that's 20 inches long or less. It'll be easier to use. Don't buy a ripsaw; it isn't designed to cut across the grain of the board.

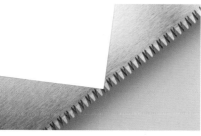

...ook like this.

...erent sets of
...n above) cut
...elow) cut neater.

Making a Crosscut

After you've marked a cut line on the board, and it's clamped firmly to the workbench, you're ready to use your saw.

1 Place the blade of the saw on the **waste side** of the cut line. (The waste side of the board is the side that isn't part of the project piece.) The saw is going to remove about 1⁄16 inch of the wood as it cuts, so it will change the length of the board if you make your cut right on the line.

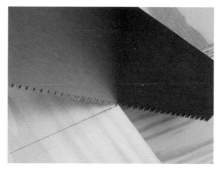

2 Set the thumb of your free hand lightly against the saw blade's side, just above the teeth.

3 Pull the saw lightly back and forth, being careful to keep the saw's teeth away from your thumb. The saw will make a little groove in the wood, called a **kerf**.

4 Move your free hand away from the saw. Put it on the board, well away from the saw's teeth. Line up your eyes, your sawing arm, and shoulder behind the blade. This position puts the power of your upper body behind the saw and will make sawing easier. Plant both feet a little apart and continue to saw.

5 As you saw back and forth, tilt the point of the saw at a 45-degree angle to the floor. Keep the blade straight up and down. (Imagine a square lining up the side of the saw with the face of the board.) Don't let it lean to the left or right. The blade will follow the cut line. Cut slowly and steadily, and take a break whenever you need one.

6 If the saw begins to wander from the cut line, guide it back by gently twisting the saw's handle very lightly as you make your cut. Keep your eyes on the marked line, and your sawing straight and true! Have your adult helper carefully support the wood that hangs over the edge of your workbench so that it doesn't tear off as you finish your saw cut.

7 Label the piece you just cut out. Use the letter listed under the Code section of the Cut List. (This will help you figure out which piece goes where when you build your project.)

Making a Rip Cut

Ripping a board is a lot like cross-cutting, except that it's easier for your saw to wobble off the line you marked. The projects in this book only require that you rip very short distances, so you can use your handsaw.

1 Clamp your board in place. The marked line should hang over the edge of your workbench.

2 Line up the blade with the mark and make a kerf in the end of the board, as you did when cross-cutting.

3 Carefully cut along the line you marked, using the same techniques you used with crosscutting. Make sure the blade cuts straight along the line.

COPING SAW

This strange-looking saw is used to cut curved lines, circles, and inside boards. (See the photo on page 10.) The blade rotates so you can cut in any direction. That's why this saw cuts oddly shaped lines and in places no other saw can reach. The saw's teeth point back toward the handle and it cuts as you pull the blade. A little pin at each end of the blade is tightly held to the frame's ends with two pin holders, creating tension. The tension allows the thin blade to cut through wood. If the handle is loosened, it won't cut correctly because the tension disappears and the blade flops around. Practice on scrap wood to get the hang of using this tool.

Cutting Curves

Sometimes it's easier to use your coping saw when the board is clamped straight up and down. Do whatever feels most comfortable.

1 Grip the saw's handle with one hand. Set the blade on the edge of the wood, even with the line that you've marked, and gently push and pull the blade across the wood. (You don't have to make a kerf with this saw.) Keep a little pressure on the blade, but don't press too hard. This will bend or break the blade. Remember, the saw cuts on the pull stroke; use just enough pressure to keep the blade in place on the push stroke.

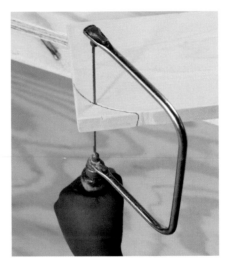

2 Watch the marked line and turn the handle slightly so that the blade follows that line. Don't turn the saw's blade too tightly to follow a curve, or the blade may bend or break. You'll get a feel for how tight your turns can be after you've made a few cuts.

3 Keep the blade of your saw aimed in the direction you want to cut, and you won't go wrong.

4 If the frame bangs against the outside of the wood, you can't continue sawing. Turn both

pin holders, turning the frame away from the wood. Then keep sawing. Do this as often as you need.

5 When you're done cutting out the piece, label it with the pencil.

Replacing the Blade

When the coping saw's blade breaks, you'll need to replace it. This can be tricky. Four hands are better than two, so ask for some adult help.

1 Look at how the two pin holders grip each end of the blade. Loosen the handle by turning it until you can remove the blade.

2 Insert a new blade onto the two pin holders, turning the teeth back toward the handle.

3 Tighten the handle so that the blade is held tightly in the frame.

Inside Cuts with a Coping Saw

1 Start by boring a hole at least ¼ inch wide just inside of the shape you want to cut out.

TIP

Now and then, you may cut a type of wood that you don't use often (such as a piece of lattice) or you'll have to make a cut that doesn't quite fit with the instructions given here. Think about how to make the cut safely and accurately. Then clamp your board securely and make the cut. Use common sense and get a little help from your adult assistant, too!

2 Remove the blade from your coping saw, slip the blade through the hole, and tighten the blade back into the saw frame. Now cut out the shape.

Building Your Project

Now that all the pieces are cut, you're ready to assemble the project. You'll nail or screw (and sometimes glue) the pieces together. The places where pieces are fastened are called **joints**. Each project has an illustration that shows how all the pieces fit together. Refer to it often as you build your project.

MAKING JOINTS

The projects in this book only use two types of joints: face joints and right-angle joints. A **face joint** is made of two boards fastened face to face. This joint is very strong. **Right-angle joints** are two boards fastened together at a 90-degree

angle. This joint is weak on its own, but when you put several right-angle joints together (as you do with a box), your project will be strong.

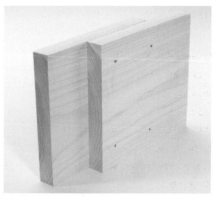
Face joint

Right-angle joint

Fasten together these joints with nails or screws. Glue helps to strengthen the joints, especially if they're going to hold weight. Each project will tell you exactly how to fasten the joints.

MAKING JOINTS FIT

No matter how carefully you cut, sometimes the pieces of your project won't fit together perfectly. One board might be a tiny bit too long, or the cut might not be straight. A **rasp** can scrape a little wood from the end of a piece to make it fit. (Unfortunately, if the piece is too short, you'll have to measure and cut a new piece.)

Using Your Rasp

A half-round rasp has a flat side to use on flat surfaces, and a curved side to use on the inside of curved saw cuts.

1 Clamp the piece securely to your bench.

2 Hold the rasp's handle in one hand, and place the teeth where you want to remove wood. Keeping the rasp flat, push it across the wood. It may be helpful to put a little pressure on the steel with the fingers of your other hand. (You'll

hold the rasp in the same position when you're shaping curved lines.)

3 A rasp only cuts away the wood as it's moving forward, so pick it up to bring it back

to the starting position. Push it forward again, lift it up, move it back, and push it forward.

4 Test the fit of the piece. When it fits, you're done.

FASTENING WITH GLUE

Wood glue (sometimes called carpenter's yellow glue) can help hold pieces of wood together when you need a really strong joint. After you glue a joint, always fasten it with nails or screws. The trick to gluing is to use the right amount of glue—enough to make the pieces stick together, but not too much! When glue drips or squeezes out from the project you're building, you've used too much. Wipe it up quickly with a damp paper towel or rag. If the drips have already started to dry, you can peel them up with your fingernails. If they're really dry, ask your adult assistant to help you get rid of them.

Gluing a Face Joint

If you want to glue the faces of two boards together, do this.

1 Run several thin lines of glue along the boards' matching faces.

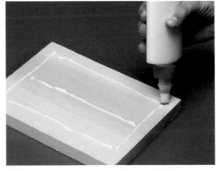

2 Set the boards together. Drive nails or screws into them.

3 Wipe up any extra glue that squeezed out. Let the glue dry. This takes about 24 hours.

Gluing a Right Angle Joint

When you glue an end or an edge of one board to another board, do it like this:

1 Run a thin line of glue along the center of the edge.

2 Set the boards together. Drive in nails or screws.

3 Wipe up any extra glue that squeezed out. Let the glue dry. This takes about 24 hours.

TIP

> Peel the dried glue off the glue bottle's tip before squeezing out a line of glue.

FASTENING WITH NAILS

You can use nails to fasten joints. They come in many types and sizes. The three types you'll need for the projects in this book are common nails, finishing nails, and brads. The project instructions will tell you what type and length of nail you'll need for each project.

Using the right length of nail is particularly important. You want the nail to be long enough to go through the first board and into the second, but not so long that it comes out the other side. Look at the photo below. The nail on the left is too long for the boards. The nail on the right is the perfect length. The only tricky thing about nails is that their length is measured two different ways: in inches and in "pennies." A 2-inch-long nail is also called a 6d nail. (The

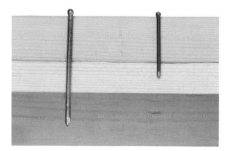

"d" stands for "penny.") Nail boxes list both measurements. The project instructions measure nails in inches rather than pennies. But here's a handy chart just in case.

Penny	Inches
3d	1¼"
4d	1½"
6d	2"
8d	2½"
10d	3"
12d	3¼"
16d	3½"

*Top: A **finishing nail** is thinner and has a small head. Use it to hammer into thin pieces of wood and when you want a neater-looking project.*

*Middle: A **common nail** has a wide head. Use it to nail together thick pieces of wood, such us two 1½ x 3½-inch boards.*

*Bottom: A **brad** is like a tiny finishing nail. Use it to nail together really thin pieces of wood.*

USING YOUR HAMMER

There are two different parts to the head of the hammer. The flattened, circular end is for pounding nails. (You can also use it to tap on a piece of wood so it lines up with another board.) The steel claw is for pulling out nails that are bent or in the wrong place.

CAUTION: Sometimes a nail will fly in the air when you hit it with your hammer, so always wear your safety glasses. Hammering well takes a little practice, but you'll get plenty of it as you build your projects.

Hammering Nails

Practice hammering with common nails and scrap wood. (The bigger head makes the nails easier to hit.) Always wear your safety glasses.

1 Grip the hammer handle with the hand you write with. The farther from the head you hold the handle, the more power you'll have (but the less control). Grip the handle wherever it feels best to you.

2 Turn the steel face of the hammer down and away from you. Line up the handle with your elbow.

3 Hold the nail in between the index finger and thumb of your other hand. Set the nail's point where you want it to enter the wood. Make sure you're holding the nail straight up and down. (Tilting the nail will make it bend or go out the side of the board when you pound it.)

4 To start the nail, tap its head several times with the hammer until the point of the nail sticks into the wood. Move your other hand away from the nail. Use it to steady the board.

5 Keep your eye on the nail's head as you swing the hammer down onto it, and hit the nail sharply. If the nail doesn't sink into the board a bit, hit it harder. Swing your hammer from the elbow and arm to use the power of your whole upper body, not just your wrist. Swing carefully and steadily.

6 When the nail is almost all the way in, start hitting it very lightly until the head is flat on the wood's surface. Try not to dent the wood with the hammer.

Pulling a Bent Nail

Sometimes a nail bends before it's driven all the way in, the tip pops

TIP

Don't try to hammer a nail through a knot in the wood— you'll just bend the nail! Be careful not to put a nail to close to the edge or end of a board. It will split the wood.

out the side of the board, or it goes in the wrong place. If this happens, pull the nail back out.

1 Grip the nail with the V-shaped slot of the hammer claw. Place the steel top of the hammer flat on the wood next to the nail, with the hammer straight up and down.

2 Use one hand to hold the board still. With the other hand, pull the handle down toward the board and away from the nail until the nail comes out.

3 If you're having a hard time, slip a piece of scrap wood between the board and the top of the hammer's head.

4 Start the nail in a new spot and try it again.

TIP

When you're trying to hammer a nail really close to the end of the board, this trick will help you avoid splitting the wood: Turn a nail upside down and dull the sharp point a little bit with a light whack or two from your hammer. Then turn the nail right-side up, position it, and pound it in. The nail will drive straight and won't split the end of the board! The nail's dulled point crushes straight through the wood's grain instead of following the grain and going at an angle. This is one case where sharper isn't always better.

CHECKING FOR A RIGHT ANGLE

After you've nailed a right-angle joint, use your square to make sure it's at a 90-degree angle.

1 Fit the square into the inside corner where the two boards meet. Press the handle against one board, and check to see whether the edge of the blade is tight against the other board.

2 If your square won't fit inside the corner of your project, hold the square tightly against the outside corner instead and check that the pieces are square.

3 If there's a space between the blade and the board, you'll need to adjust the assembled boards a bit so the joint is square. Use your hammer to tap lightly on one of the boards in the direction it needs to go. Check the joint for square again.

FASTENING WITH SCREWS

A screw fastens joints like a nail, but goes in a little differently. The threads grip the wood tightly, so it's a little more secure than a nail. The first thing you'll need to do is use the electric drill to bore a **pilot hole**. This will help keep your screw from splitting the wood. Then you'll use your screwdriver to drive the screw into the joint.

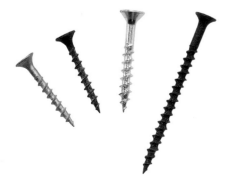

There are many types, thicknesses, and lengths of screws. The projects in this book use flathead Phillips screws. They're the easiest kind of screw to put in, and the head fits flat against the wood. The Phillips screw has two slots that cross to make an X shape on its head.

Screws are sized by their thickness (No. 6, No. 8, No. 10, and so on; the smaller the number, the smaller the screw), and by their length. For these projects, the Shopping List will tell you which screws you'll need.

USING AN ELECTRIC DRILL

The electric drill is the only power tool you'll use regularly when making these projects. The drill bores holes in the wood. Have your adult assistant help until you feel completely comfortable with this tool. The drill has a trigger, which turns it on and off. (Some drills drill at different speeds, depending on how hard you press the trigger.)

The chuck is a circular sleeve that holds the bit. The bit is a small metal piece that goes into the wood. Bits come in different sizes: the larger the bit, the larger the hole will be. The drill also has a button that reverses the direction the bit spins. You'll use this button to back the drill out of the hole after you finish drilling.

Chucking a Bit

When you put a bit into your drill it's called **chucking**.

1 Grip the drill with one hand and rotate the chuck with your other hand until the jaws open. (Rotate the chuck in both directions to see how the jaws work.)

2 Slip the end of the bit without the spiral grooves into the jaws. It should go in about ½ inch.

3 Rotate the chuck in the opposite direction to tighten the jaws onto the end of the bit. Have your adult helper make sure the chuck is completely tightened.

TIP

Some drills have a chuck key, a small tool used to loosen and tighten the chuck. Insert the key into a hole in the chuck. Twisting the key will loosen and tighten the chuck.

Dimpling the Pilot Hole

Before you drill a hole, dimple the mark for your drill's bit. This will help keep the bit from slipping around on the board.

1 Set the tip of a large nail on the mark where the hole goes. Tap the nail lightly once or twice with your hammer.

2 Remove the nail. There's your dimple!

Drilling the Pilot Hole

Now you're ready to drill.

1 Put on your safety glasses.

2 Set the dimpled board flat on your workbench.

3 Slip a piece of scrap wood beneath the board, and then clamp the "sandwich" to your workbench. The scrap wood will keep you from drilling holes into your workbench.

TIP

If your bit slips in the chuck as you drill a hole, stop and tighten the chuck securely.

4 Set the tip of the bit in the dimpled layout. Hold the drill straight up and down.

5 Squeeze the drill's trigger to begin drilling. Apply pressure straight down to drive the bit into the wood.

6 Stop drilling when the bit pops through the bottom of the board. You'll feel this happen as the bit enters the second board, or comes out the other side if the board is hanging over the edge of the workbench.

7 Reverse the drill direction to back the bit out.

Flagging a Bit

Sometimes you want to drill a hole that doesn't go all the way through the board. Use a piece of tape to show you when to stop drilling.

1 Lay your bit on your workbench.

2 Use your measuring tape to measure the depth of the hole on the length of the bit, starting from the tip.

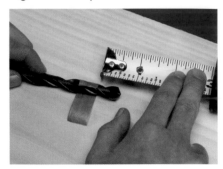

3 Wrap the end of a piece of masking tape around the bit, so the edge of the tape is at the depth you want to drill. Let the other end of the tape stick out like a flag.

4 Chuck the bit into your drill, dimple the hole, and drill it. Stop drilling when the edge of the flag touches the face of the board. Reverse the drill to back the bit out.

SCREWDRIVERS

Screwdrivers are used to drive screws into wood. There are two different types of screwdrivers. Each has a different tip. The flattened tip of a standard screwdriver is used to drive slotted-head screws. The X-shaped tip of a Phillips screwdriver fits into the X on the head of a Phillips screw. Since the projects in this book use Phillips screws, make sure you get a Phillips screwdriver. Screwdriver tips come in different sizes. Get a No. 2 tip. It's medium-sized and will work well with all the screws you'll use in the projects.

How to Drive a Screw

After you've bored the pilot hole, you're ready to drive the screw.

1 Set the screw's point into the pilot hole. Then set the screwdriver's tip into the X-shaped slot on the head of the screw.

2 Turn the screwdriver clockwise, using the power in your shoulder to drive in the screw. Keep the screwdriver's tip centered in the head of the screw so that it won't slip out.

3 To back the screw out, turn the screwdriver counterclockwise.

Finishing Touches

You didn't think you were done, did you? There's one last, very important step: finishing! This makes your projects look and feel great, and protects them so they'll last a long time. First you'll sand the project. Then you'll paint, varnish, or stain it. Each **finish** gives wood a different appearance, but the main job of finish is to protect the wood and seal out dirt and dampness.

When the weather's good, finish your project outdoors. If you have to work indoors, be sure that there's plenty of fresh air in your workshop, and stay far away from any sources of heat or open flame.

SANDING

Sanding smoothes out any rough spots on your project and prepares the wood surface for finishing. Because sanding creates a lot of floating sawdust, always wear a paper dust-mask to help keep it out of your lungs.

There are many kinds of sandpaper, but for this book's projects, you'll use 100- and 180-grit garnet sandpaper. Sandpaper **grit** gets

smaller in size as the grit number increases, so 100-grit is rougher than 180-grit. You'll use the 100-grit sandpaper to take off the rough spots. Then you'll use the 180-grit sandpaper to smooth everything out. (You can substitute another kind of sandpaper if you can't find garnet, but get both grit sizes.)

Sanding sponges are soft rubbery blocks coated with sandpaper grit. You can use one of these if you like. They're great for sanding curving edges made with your coping saw and your rasp.

Your rasp (see the photo on page 10) is perfect for sanding inside holes, around curves, and other places the sandpaper won't reach easily. It's also great for taking off the teeth marks your saw left on the ends of boards.

How to Sand Your Project

Your goal is to get rid of all the rough spots and sharp edges. Always wear your paper dust mask when sanding.

1 Fold the 100-grit sandpaper in quarters. Unfold it and then tear along the creases to get smaller pieces.

2 Hold a piece of sandpaper and rub the grit across the wood. Whenever you can, rub in the same direction as the wood grain. This gives a smoother surface than rubbing across the grain.

3 Sand the edges, ends, corners, and faces of every piece of your project.

4 Wipe the sawdust off and run your fingers over every part of your project, checking for rough spots. Look at it closely under a good light. If you see or feel any rough spots, sand them smooth.

5 Wipe the sawdust off, then repeat steps 1 through 4 with the 180-grit sandpaper. This will make the surface extra smooth.

PAINTS, VARNISHES, AND STAINS

To make your projects look their best and to help them last as long as possible, apply a finish. There are several finishes to choose from: paint, varnish, and stain. The type of finish you choose depends on how you want your project to look. This final step seals the wood, protecting it from dirt and moisture.

Once you put finish on your project, it will last a long time. Each of the projects in this book recommends a way to finish it.

Buy the best paintbrushes you can afford and take good care of them by cleaning the brushes immediately after using them. Inexpensive brushes leave behind a trail of sticky hairs. With the few brushes listed on page 9, you can complete every painting and staining job in this book.

CHOOSING PAINT

Get paint in any color you want. Use **semigloss** or flat, latex enamel paint. Latex enamel paint is water-based, which means it cleans up with warm water. Semigloss (sometimes called satin) paint is sort of shiny. Flat paint isn't shiny at all. High-gloss paint shows every little imperfection on your projects, and who wants that?

If you plan to use your project outdoors, look for the word exterior on the paint can's label. If your project is going to stay indoors, choose an interior paint instead. Before you paint, prime the wood. **Primer** seals the wood and raises the grain. It makes a nice surface for the paint to stick to.

TIP

Applying primer and paint to every surface of your project is easier than it sounds. First, prime the top and sides. Let the primer dry. Then flip the project so it rests on its top. Prime the bottom. Use the same technique to apply paint.

Priming

Before you grab your paintbrushes, wipe every speck of sawdust and dirt from your workbench and your project with a damp rag. If dust sticks to the finish, it will ruin the smooth surface.

1 Cover your workbench with newspapers. Set your project on top of a few pieces of scrap wood so that it isn't touching the newspaper. (If it's touching, the newspaper will stick to your project when the primer dries.)

2 Put some clean rags and a bucket of water nearby to clean up spills and wipe off your hands.

3 Open the can of primer. Stir it with a clean piece of scrap wood.

4 Dip the tip of your brush into the primer, wiping off extra paint on the side of the paint can. (If you put too much primer on your brush, it will drip.) Brush it on to the project. Brush with the grain, covering the project with an even coat. Let the primer dry.

5 Sand the project again with the 180-grit sandpaper. (The primer soaks into the wood and raises the grain, making the surface rough, so don't skip this step!)

Applying Paint

After you've primed and sanded your project, it's time to paint it.

1. Lay out newspaper and scrap wood on your workbench, just as you did to prime the project.

2. Put some clean rags and a bucket of water nearby for cleaning up spills and wiping off your hands.

3. Open the can of paint. Stir it up with a piece of clean scrap wood.

4. Dip the tip of your brush into the paint. If you put too much paint on your brush, it will drip. Brush it onto the project. Brush with the grain, covering the project with an even coat of paint.

5. Let the paint dry. Then repeat step 4 to add another coat of paint. Always use at least two coats of paint.

CHOOSING STAIN AND VARNISH

Stain and varnish are finishes that let the grain of the wood show

TIP

If you're painting multiple colors, start with the lightest shade. Let the paint dry before painting the next color.

through. Look for water-based kinds—they're easier to clean up and a lot less toxic. When you use either of these products, read the can carefully for any additional instructions.

Applying Stain

Stain makes the wood a slightly different color.

1. To see what your stain will look like before you apply it to your project, brush some on a scrap of the same wood as you used for the project. The more coats of stain you put on, the darker the wood will become, so go easy until you're sure how much to use!

2. Paint the stain on your project. (You don't need to prime or seal the wood first. The stain soaks in.)

3. Sand everything with 180-grit sandpaper when the stain is dry.

4. Apply two coats of varnish to seal the project.

Applying Varnish

Semigloss or satin varnish gives your wood a nice glow.

1. After you've finished sanding the project, apply a coat of sanding sealer. Then follow the instructions for priming.

2. When the sanding sealer is dry, add two coats of varnish. (Follow the instructions for painting.)

TIP

Never store your paintbrushes standing on their bristles. The weight of the handle will bend the bristles. Lay them on a shelf or other flat surface.

Cleaning Your Brushes

Your paintbrushes will last a long time if you clean them well immediately after you use them.

1. Dip the paintbrush in warm water. Squeeze the bristles.

2. Gently run your fingernails along the bristles of the brush. Don't bend the bristles in ways they don't want to go.

3. Repeat steps 1 and 2 until all the finish is removed. Change the water whenever you need to.

4. Set the paintbrush on its side to dry.

You're Finished!

Ready to try out your new skills? Turn the page and start building a few tools for your workshop.

Miter Box

The perfect tool for making perfectly square saw cuts.

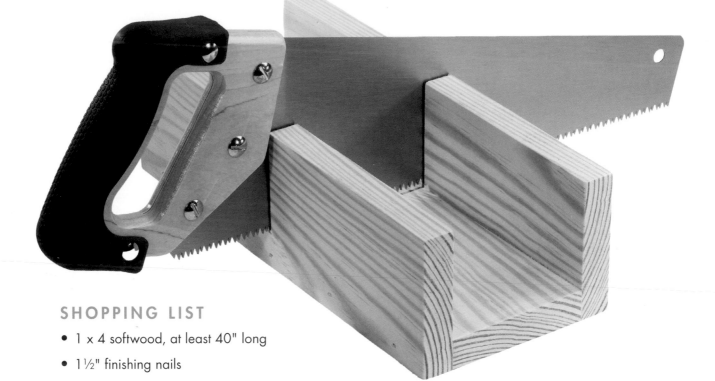

SHOPPING LIST

- 1 x 4 softwood, at least 40" long
- 1½" finishing nails

TOOLS

- Layout tools
- Clamps
- Handsaw
- Hammer
- Wood glue
- 100-grit sandpaper

CUT LIST

Code	Part	Number	Size	Material
A	Base	1	¾" x 3½" x 12"	Softwood
B	Fence	1	¾" x 3½" x 12"	Softwood
C	Front	1	¾" x 3½" x 12"	Softwood

EXPLODED VIEW

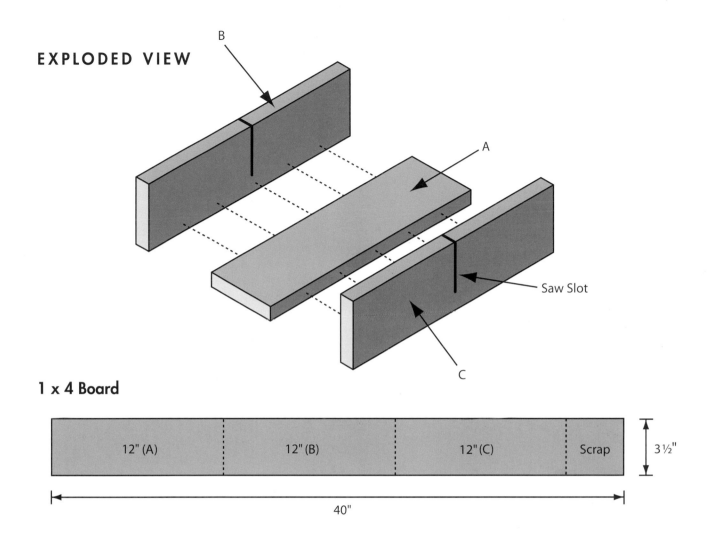

B

A

Saw Slot

C

1 x 4 Board

12" (A)	12" (B)	12"(C)	Scrap

3½"

40"

Cutting the Pieces

1 First you'll lay out and cut your pieces. Measure and mark your 1 x 4 board as shown in the board diagram above. All three pieces will be 12 inches long.

2 Clamp the board so the first layout mark hangs over the edge of the workbench. Use your handsaw to cut along the line. Label the base (A) and set it aside.

3 Now repeat steps 1 and 2 to lay out, clamp, and cut the fence (B) and front (C). Don't forget to label the pieces.

Building the Box

4 Assembling your miter box is pretty easy, but you'll need an adult to help you hold everything together. You're going to attach the fence (B) and front (C) to the base (A).

5 Have your adult helper stand the base (A) on its edge. Run a thin line of glue along the edge. Set the fence (B) on top of the edge of the base so that it makes an L shape. Line up the edges and the ends of both pieces.

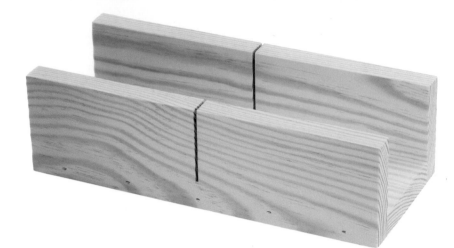

TIP

This miter box will only cut pieces of wood that are less than 3½ inches wide. If you want to cut wider boards, use a wider board to make the base (A).

6 While your adult helper holds the pieces tightly together, hammer five 1½-inch finishing nails through the fence (B) and into the edge of the base (A). Space the nails about 2 inches apart.

7 Flip the L-shaped piece so it rests on the face of the fence (B). Repeat steps 5 and 6 to glue and nail the front (C) to the other edge of the base.

Cutting a Saw Slot

8 Start by finding the center point of the fence (B). On the top edge of the fence, measure and mark a spot 6 inches from the end.

9 Repeat step 8 for the front (C) of the miter box.

10 Lay the square across the two marks. Press the handle of the square tightly against the face of the fence (B). Draw a line along the edge of the square with your pencil, marking the top edges of the fence and the front (C).

11 Now you're going to mark the cut lines on the inside face of the fence (B). Set the square inside the miter box, so its bottom edge rests on the base (A). Slide it over until its arm is lined up with the mark on the top edge of the fence. Use your pencil to mark a line along the face of the fence.

12 Move the square to the front (C) of the miter box, touching its outside face. Slide the square until its arm touches the line you made in step 10. Use your pencil to mark a line down the front. Now you have two cut lines: one on the inside face of the fence (B) and one on the outside face of the front.

13 Clamp the miter box. With your adult helper, carefully cut through the cut lines on the front (C) and fence (B). Stop cutting when you reach the base.

Finishing Touches

14 Sand your miter box. Wipe off the sawdust.

Using the Miter Box

15 You'll use your miter box to make perfectly square cuts in smaller pieces of wood. It's also great for holding dowels. (Don't ever try to hold a round dowel in place with a clamp—it will slip.)

16 Clamp the miter box in place. Set the piece of wood you want to cut inside. Line up the cut line with the saw slot.

17 Pick up the saw. With your other hand, press the wood against the fence (B). Slip the saw blade into the slot and saw away.

Estimated Time: 3 hours

Toolbox

Every woodworker needs a toolbox!

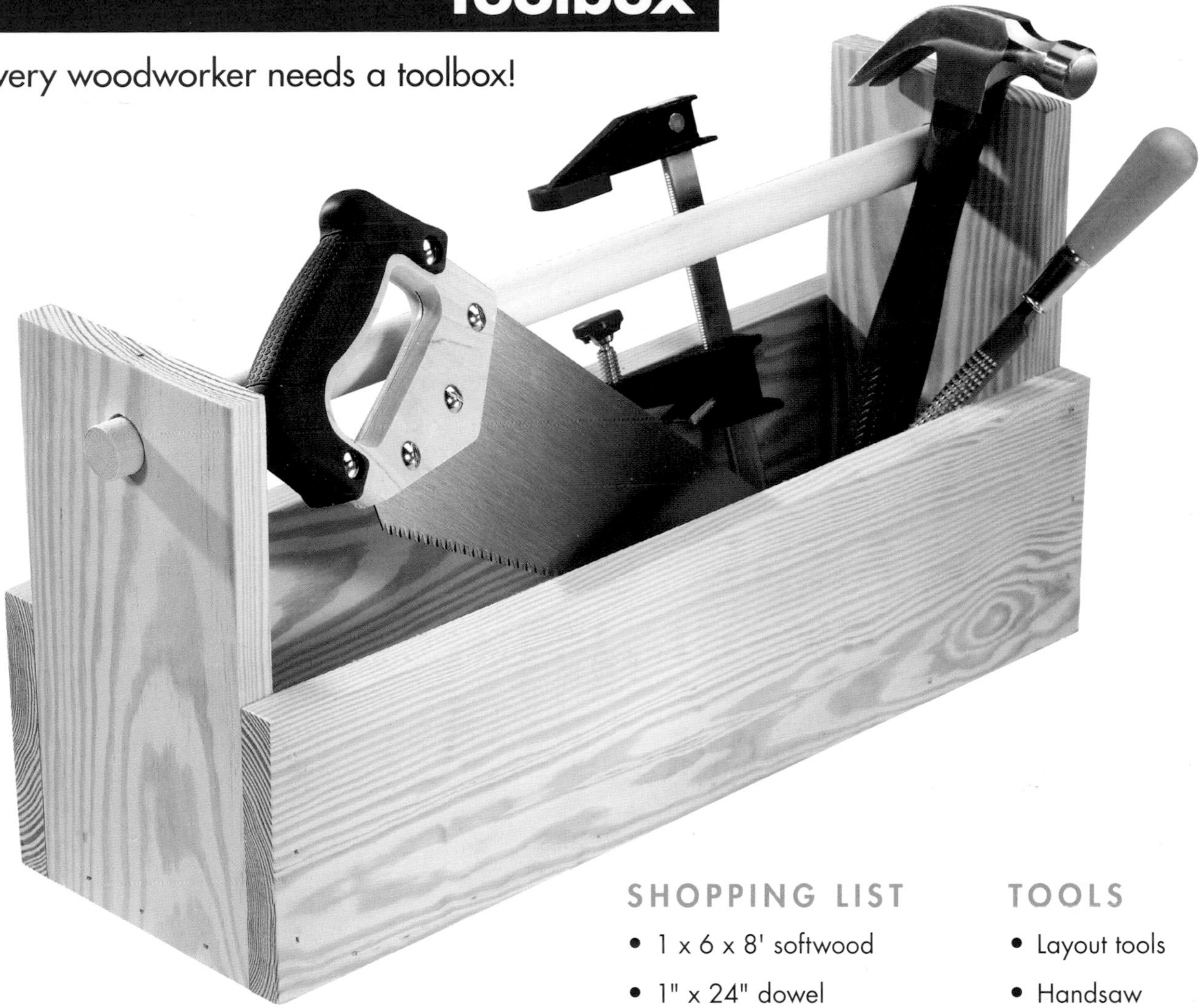

SHOPPING LIST

- 1 x 6 x 8' softwood
- 1" x 24" dowel
- 1½" and 2" finishing nails
- 100-grit and 180-grit sandpaper

TOOLS

- Layout tools
- Handsaw
- Miter box
- Clamps
- Hammer
- Drill with 1" bit
- Wood glue

CUT LIST

Code	Part	Number	Size	Material
A	Bottom	1	¾" x 5½" x 19½"	Softwood
B	Side	2	¾" x 5½" x 21"	Softwood
C	End	2	¾" x 5½" x 11"	Softwood
D	Handle	1	1" x 22"	Dowel

EXPLODED VIEW

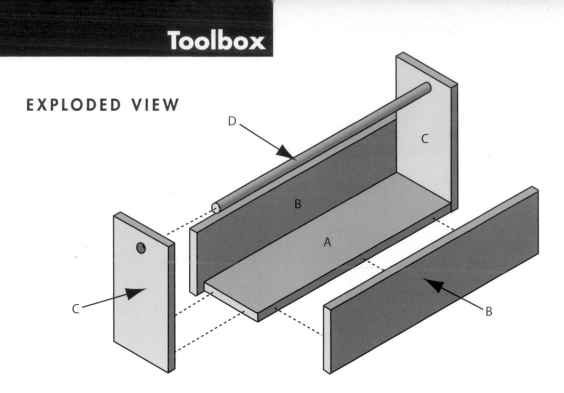

1 x 6 Board

19½" (A)	21" (B)	21" (B)	11" (C)	11" (C)	Scrap

5½"

8'

Figure A

2¾"

1½"

End (C)

Cutting and Drilling

1 Lay out, cut, and label the bottom (A), sides (B), and ends (C) from your 1 x 6 board. Use the diagram above to help you lay out the board.

2 Lay out the dowel and use the miter box to cut it to make the handle piece (D).

3 On the face of one end (C) piece, make a mark that is 2¾ inches from the edge and 1½ inches from the end. See Figure A for help. This is where the handle (D) will go.

4 Place a piece of scrap wood beneath the first end (C) piece and then clamp the two pieces to your workbench. Chuck the 1-inch bit into your drill. Dimple the mark you made in step 3. Drill through the mark to make the handle (D) hole.

5 Repeat steps 3 and 4 to drill another hole through the other end (C) piece.

Starting from the Bottom

6 Run a line of glue along on 5½-inch end of the bottom (A). Stand the piece on its opposite end.

7 Using the end opposite the handle hole, set the first end (C) piece on top of the glued end of the bottom (A). Line up the edges of both pieces to form an L shape.

8 While your adult helper holds the pieces together, hammer three 2-inch nails through the end (C) and into the end of the bottom (A). Space the nails about 1½ inches apart.

9 To attach the other end (C), flip the L shape so it rests on the face of the end you just attached. Repeat steps 6 through 8 to attach the other end. Now you have a C-shape.

Adding the Sides

10 Lay the C-shape on its side, so it's resting on the edges of the bottom (A) and the ends (C). Run a thin line of glue along the edge of the bottom and 5 inches up the edge of each end piece. (Don't glue more than 5 inches up each end. The side of the toolbox won't go up any higher than that.)

11 Set the first side (B) on top of the glue and line up the edges. While your adult helper holds the pieces together, hammer a row of 2-inch nails through the face of the side and into the edges of the ends (C) and bottom (A). Space the nails on the bottom about 4 inches apart. The nails on the sides should be 2 inches apart.

12 To attach the other side, flip the assembly upside down so it rests on the face of the side (B) you just attached. Repeat steps 10 and 11 to attach the other side.

Inserting the Handle

13 Set the toolbox upright. Slide the handle (D) through the first hole in the end (C) and then into the second. Make sure the ends of the handle stick out ½ inch beyond the outside faces of the ends.

14 While your adult helper holds the handle (D) in place, hammer a 1½-inch nail through the center of the top edge of the end (C), so it goes into the handle. Hammer another nail into the other end piece.

Finishing Touches

15 Sand the toolbox. Wipe off the sawdust. Load up your tools!

Compass Tool

Make a simple compass for drawing circles on your layouts.
It can also double as a straight edge.

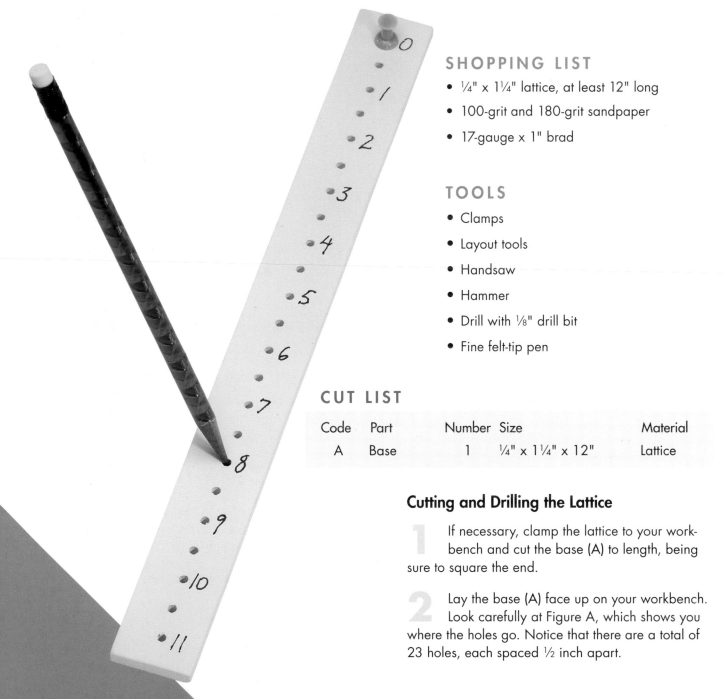

SHOPPING LIST

- ¼" x 1¼" lattice, at least 12" long
- 100-grit and 180-grit sandpaper
- 17-gauge x 1" brad

TOOLS

- Clamps
- Layout tools
- Handsaw
- Hammer
- Drill with ⅛" drill bit
- Fine felt-tip pen

CUT LIST

Code	Part	Number	Size	Material
A	Base	1	¼" x 1¼" x 12"	Lattice

Cutting and Drilling the Lattice

1 If necessary, clamp the lattice to your workbench and cut the base (A) to length, being sure to square the end.

2 Lay the base (A) face up on your workbench. Look carefully at Figure A, which shows you where the holes go. Notice that there are a total of 23 holes, each spaced ½ inch apart.

Figure A

Use your measuring tape to find the center of each end of the base (A), and mark the points.

4 With your square, draw a straight line connecting the two marks you just made.

5 Hook your measuring tape over one end of the base (A). Stretch the tape along the board's length, and make a mark every ½ inch on the centerline you drew in step 4. These are your hole marks.

6 Lightly tap the center of each hole mark with a hammer and nail. This starter hole will help you drill exact holes in the next steps.

7 Set a piece of scrap wood under the base (A). Clamp both pieces of wood to the workbench.

8 Chuck a ⅛-inch bit in your drill. Drill through each starter hole you made in step 6. The lattice is really thin, so don't press down hard on the drill. Its weight should do all the work for you.

Finishing Touches

9 Sand the compass tool well. It's okay to sand off the penciled layout lines. Wipe off the sawdust.

10 If you'd like, prime and paint your compass tool.

11 Use a fine felt-tip pen to label the holes. Label the first hole 0", the next one ½", then 1", and so on.

Using the Compass

12 To mark a circle or semicircle on a piece of wood, use your tape measure and a pencil to mark the center on the wood's face. (Or the center of where you want the circle to go.)

13 Lightly hammer a brad into the mark. Stop hammering when it's about halfway in. You'll take this brad out later.

14 Slip the 0" hole in the compass over the brad. (If the wood is soft enough, you can use a thumbtack instead of a brad.)

15 The instructions for the project will tell you the radius of the circular shape. (The radius measures from the center to the outside edge of the circle.) This is the distance from the 0" borehole (the center of the circle) to the hole you'll stick your pencil in. For instance, a 3-inch radius will use the hole marked 3". If you don't find a radius listed in the instructions, the exact size of the circle isn't important for that project.

16 Insert the tip of a sharp pencil in the correct hole. To make the circle, start drawing with the pencil. The compass will swing around on the brad in a circle.

17 If the layout isn't where you want it to be, adjust the position of the brad and try again.

18 When you're finished marking the circle, take the compass tool off the brad. Then use your hammer to remove the brad.

19 Now cut the circle you just made.

Estimated Time: 1 to 1½ hours

Bench Hook

Build this tool to help you saw. It holds small pieces of lumber in place so you don't have to clamp them.

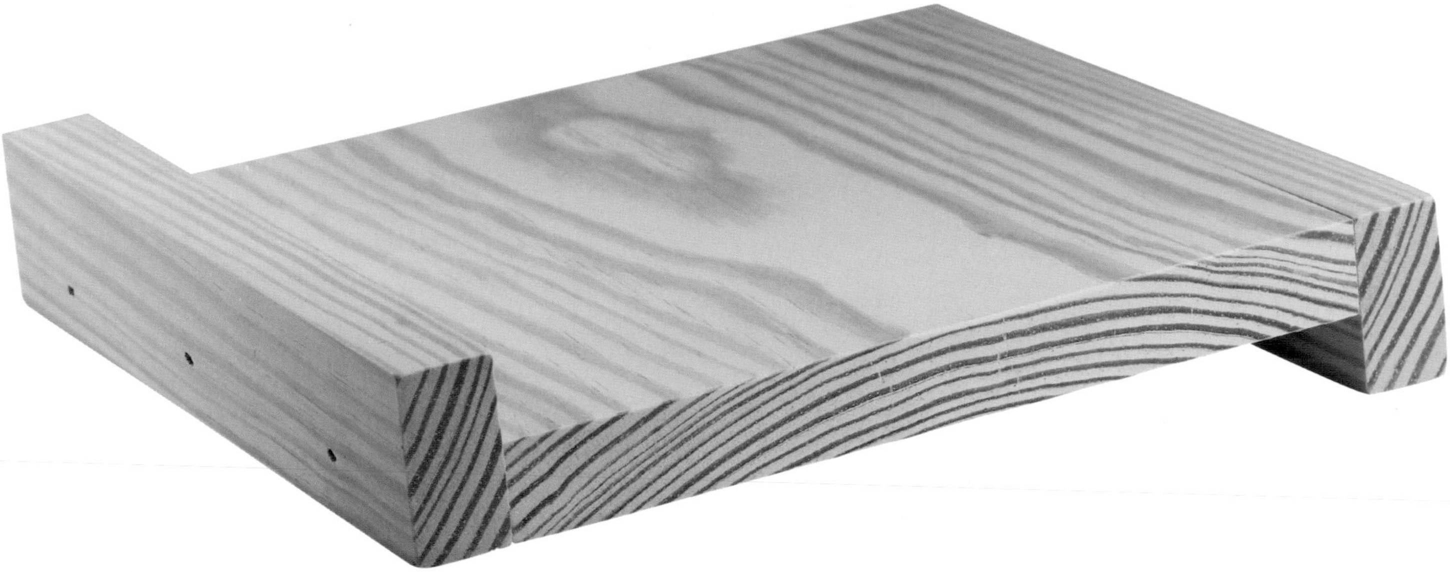

SHOPPING LIST

- 1 x 8 softwood, at least 12" long
- 1 x 2 softwood, at least 24" long
- 1½" finishing nails
- 100-grit sandpaper

TOOLS

- Layout tools
- Handsaw
- Wood glue
- Hammer

CUT LIST

Code	Part	Number	Size	Material
A	Base	1	¾" x 7¼" x 8"	Softwood
B	Fence	1	¾" x 1½" x 8"	Softwood
C	Stop	1	¾" x 1½" x 8"	Softwood

EXPLODED VIEW

B

A

C

TIP

Your bench hook works best with smaller boards and dowels that fit easily on it. For boards longer than 2 feet or wider than the base, use clamps to secure the board directly to your workbench before cutting them.

Building the Bench Hook

1 Lay out and cut the pieces for the base (A), fence (B), and stop (C). Label the pieces.

2 Ask your adult helper to stand the base (A) on one of its 8-inch ends.

3 Run a thin line of glue along the top end of the base (A). Then set the fence (B) on top of the base. Line up the two 8-inch sides to form a corner (see the Exploded View).

4 Hammer three nails through the fence (B) and into the end of the base (A). Space the nails about 2 inches apart.

5 Flip the assembly so that it rests on the fence (B). Repeat steps 3 and 4 to glue and nail the stop (C) in place. Make sure the stop hangs off the opposite side of the base (see the Exploded View).

Finishing Touches

6 Sand your bench hook well. Brush off the sawdust and you're done!

Using the Bench Hook

7 Lay the bench hook flat on your workbench with the stop (C) hooked over the edge of the workbench.

8 If you're right-handed, move the bench hook so it's even with the right front corner of the workbench. If you're a lefty, move it so it's even with the left corner.

9 Lay the board or dowel you want to cut on your bench hook. Move the board or dowel so the cut line hangs over the edge of the bench hook (just like when you clamp a board to the workbench). Press the board firmly against the fence with the heel of your hand. Pick up your saw with your other hand. Now cut the board.

Weekend Workbench

Build it this weekend and—presto! You have a workshop.
Then use it every time you do woodworking.

SHOPPING LIST

- (4) 2 x 4 x 8'
  softwood

- (1) ¾" x 4' x 8'
  plywood*

- 3¼" common nails

- 1½" finishing nails

- (8) ⅜" x 3½" plated
  carriage bolts with
  washers and wing nuts

- 100-grit and 180-grit
  sandpaper

TOOLS

- Layout tools

- Handsaw

- Hammer

- Drill with ⅜" bit

*Have someone at your lumberyard
cut the four plywood pieces to size for
you. Use the cut lines in the 4' x 8'
plywood illustration to help you. Be
sure to label each piece.*

CUT LIST

Code	Part	Number	Size	Material
A	Leg	4	1½" x 3½" x 29¼"	Softwood
B	Leg brace	4	1½" x 3½" x 21"	Softwood
C	Long brace	4	1½" x 3½" x 43⅝"	Softwood
D	Top	1	¾" x 2' x 4'	Plywood
E	Shelf top	1	¾" x 2' x 4'	Plywood
F	Side panel	2	¾" x 2' x 2'	Plywood

EXPLODED VIEW

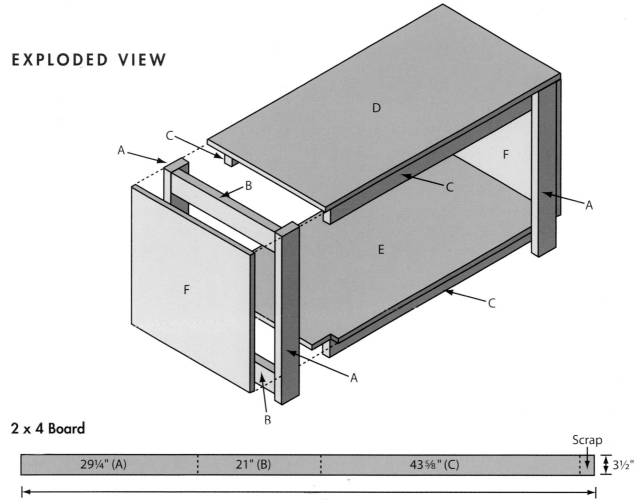

2 x 4 Board

Scrap

29¼" (A)	21" (B)	43⅝" (C)

3½"

8'

4' x 8' Plywood Board

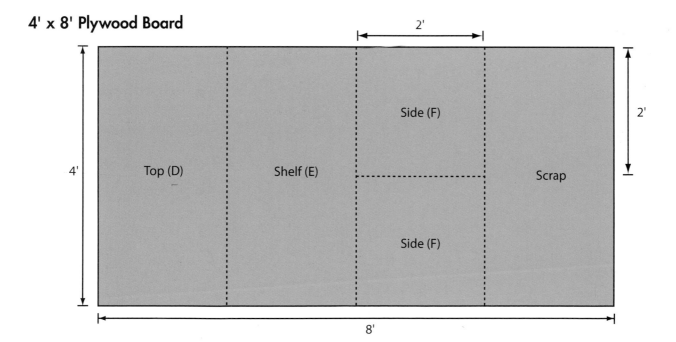

2'

Side (F)

2'

4'

Top (D) | Shelf (E)

Side (F)

Scrap

8'

Building the Sides

1 You'll assemble the sides of the workbench first. Measure and mark each of your four 2 x 4s as shown in the diagram on page 37.

2 Cut all of the pieces. Label each one and set the long braces (C) aside. The legs (A) and the leg braces (B) will form a box that the side panels (F) attach to. You'll start by making this box.

3 Have your adult helper stand one of the leg braces (B) on end. Hold a leg (A) face up on top of the leg brace, lining up the pieces as shown in Figure A. With your adult helper holding the pieces tightly together, hammer two common nails through the face of the leg into the end of the leg brace. Space the nails 1½ inches apart.

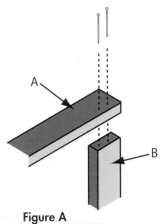

Figure A

4 Flip the assembly so that the other end of the leg brace (B) is facing up. Line up the second leg (A) with the brace as you did in step 3. Hammer two common nails through the face of the leg and into the end of the leg brace. Space the nails 1½ inches apart.

5 Measure and mark a line on the bottom end of each leg (A), 1⅛ inches from the end. Line up the second leg brace (B) so its top edge lines up with the marks you just made. While your adult helper holds the pieces in place, hammer two common nails through the face of one leg into the end of the leg brace. Space the nails 1½ inches apart. Hammer two common nails through the face of the other leg and into the other end of the leg brace. Now you have a box!

6 Lay the box down so it rests on the edges of the legs (A). The leg braces (B) should be suspended, not resting on the floor. Set one of the side panels (F) on top of the box. Line up the side panel edges with the faces of the legs. The top edge of the side panel should align with the edge of the upper leg brace. (The upper brace is the one lined up with the ends of the legs.)

7 While your adult helper holds the pieces together, hammer a row of finishing nails through the face of the side panel (F) into the edges of the legs (A) and the faces of the leg braces (B). Space the nails 4 inches apart. Congratulations! You've built the first side.

8 Now repeat steps 3 through 7 to build the second side.

Adding the Shelf

9 Set the shelf top (E) flat on your work surface. You're going to mark cutouts on this piece so that it will fit around the legs (A). Measure the bottom end of a leg (it should be about 1½ x 3½ inches). Using your square and a pencil, draw a shape exactly that size on each corner of the piece of plywood (see Figure B).

10 While your adult helper holds the shelf top (E) steady, use your handsaw to cut out the four corners along the lines you drew.

11 Now you'll build the shelf by attaching two long braces (C) to the shelf top (E). Lay two of the long braces on their edges, parallel to one another. Measure from one inside face to the other at each end, spacing them 18 inches apart.

12 With your adult assistant's help, lay the shelf top (E) on top of the long braces (C). Line up the notches in the shelf top with the outside faces of the long braces. Both ends of the shelf top should overhang the ends of the long braces by

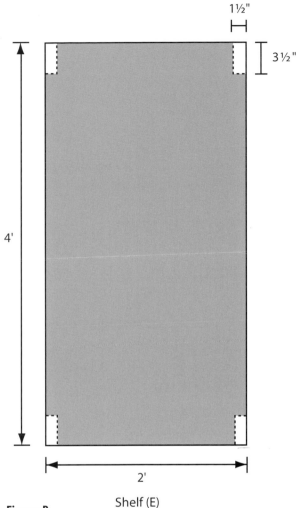

1½"

3½"

4'

2'

Figure B

Shelf (E)

Topping It Off

14 Now you can build the top, attaching the two remaining long braces (C) to the top (D). Lay two of the long braces on their edges, parallel to one another. Measure from one inside face to the other, spacing them 18 inches apart.

15 With your adult assistant's help, lay the top (D) on top of the long braces (C). The ends of the top should overhang the ends of the long braces by 2⅛ inches. The sides of the top should overhang the faces of the long braces by 1½ inches. Use your measuring tape to make sure the top is lined up properly. If the top isn't positioned correctly, it will be hard to fit the workbench together.

16 While your adult helper holds the pieces together, hammer a row of finishing nails through the face of the top (D) into the edge of both long braces (C). Space the nails about 4 inches apart.

Putting It All Together

17 Are you ready to put the workbench together? You may need two adult helpers to help with this first part. Stand the side sections upright, about 5 feet away from each other. The side panels (F) should face away from each other.

18 Slide one end of the shelf with the notches into one of the sides. The shelf will rest on the lower leg brace (B), with the notches tight against the legs (A). Then slide the other side section into the other end of the shelf until you have a good fit.

19 With your adult helpers' assistance, put the top in place. Its ends will rest on top of the upper leg braces (B), and its edges will rest on the ends of the legs (A).

2⅛ inches. Check this distance with your measuring tape. If the shelf top isn't positioned correctly, it will be hard to fit the workbench together.

13 While your adult helper holds the pieces together, hammer a row of finishing nails through the face of the shelf top (E) into the edge of a long brace (C). Space the nails about 4 inches apart. Hammer a second row of nails through the face of the shelf top on the opposite side and into the edge of the other long brace.

20 The top, shelf, and side sections are held together with carriage bolts. These bolts make the workbench sturdy. You'll need to drill eight pilot holes through the faces of the legs (A) and into the long braces (C).

21 Measure and mark the pilot holes near the top (D) and on the outside face of all four legs (A) first. Measure 2½ inches down from the ends of the legs and 2½ inches from the edge. Mark the spot on each leg.

22 Chuck the ⅜-inch bit into your drill. While your adult helpers hold the sides (F) and top (D) in place, dimple the spot you marked in step 21. Drill a pilot hole through the leg (A) face and into the long brace (C) holding the top.

23 Repeat step 22 to drill pilot holes through the ends of the other three legs (A) and into the long braces (C).

24 Now you'll drill the pilot holes through the bottom of the legs (A) and the lower long braces (B). Measure and mark pilot holes on the faces of all four legs near the bottom. Measure 2½

inches up from the ends of the legs and 2½ inches from the edge. Mark the spot on each leg.

25 Repeat steps 22 through 24 to drill the pilot holes in the lower legs (A) and into the long braces (C) holding the shelf top (E).

26 Put the first carriage bolt into the first pilot hole. (It doesn't matter which one you put in first.) It will go into the leg (A) and through the long brace (C). Tap its head with the hammer if it won't slide in easily. Put the washer and wing nut on the other end of the bolt. Tighten the wing nut. Put a carriage bolt in each pilot hole.

Finishing Touches

27 Sand your workbench.

28 Set up your workbench in the shop. As you use it, tighten the wing nuts now and then to keep it rock-solid. You've built the heart of your workshop. Well done!

Look-Inside Birdhouse

The top of this birdhouse lifts off. That makes it easy to clean out the nesting materials after the baby birds have flown away.

SHOPPING LIST

- 1 x 6 x 36" softwood
- 1 x 8 x 12" softwood
- ⅜" x 12" dowel
- 1¼" finishing nails
- 100-grit and 180-grit sandpaper
- Latex primer and paints
- 3' length of #200 twist chain (a ¼" rope could be used instead)
- Wire (optional)

TOOLS

- Layout tools
- Handsaw
- Clamps
- Drill with ⅜" and 1¼" bits*
- Rasp
- Miter box
- 1" paintbrush

This birdhouse's doorway is the perfect size for a house wren or a downy woodpecker. Before you begin this project, visit your library. Find out what birds live in your area, and what size doorway they prefer. Then use a different bit size to drill the doorway if local birds prefer a larger or smaller door.

Look-Inside Birdhouse

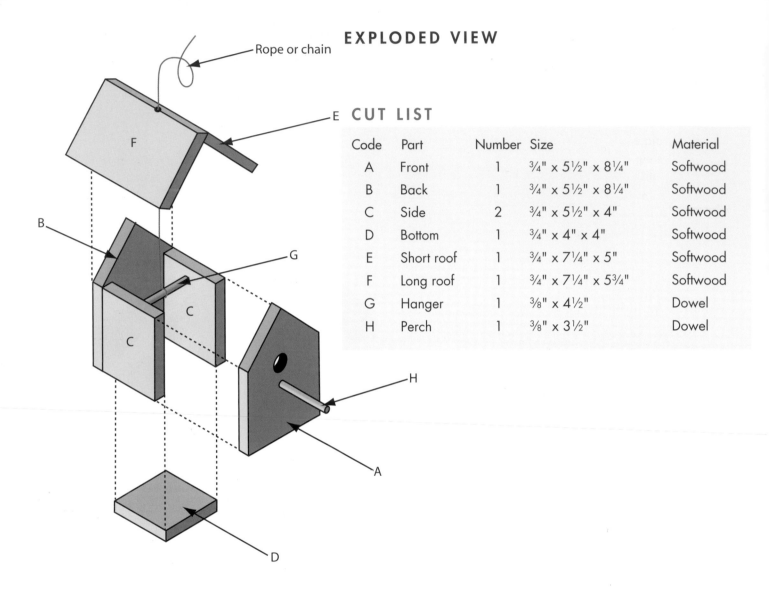

EXPLODED VIEW

Rope or chain

CUT LIST

Code	Part	Number	Size	Material
A	Front	1	¾" x 5½" x 8¼"	Softwood
B	Back	1	¾" x 5½" x 8¼"	Softwood
C	Side	2	¾" x 5½" x 4"	Softwood
D	Bottom	1	¾" x 4" x 4"	Softwood
E	Short roof	1	¾" x 7¼" x 5"	Softwood
F	Long roof	1	¾" x 7¼" x 5¾"	Softwood
G	Hanger	1	⅜" x 4½"	Dowel
H	Perch	1	⅜" x 3½"	Dowel

1 x 6 Board

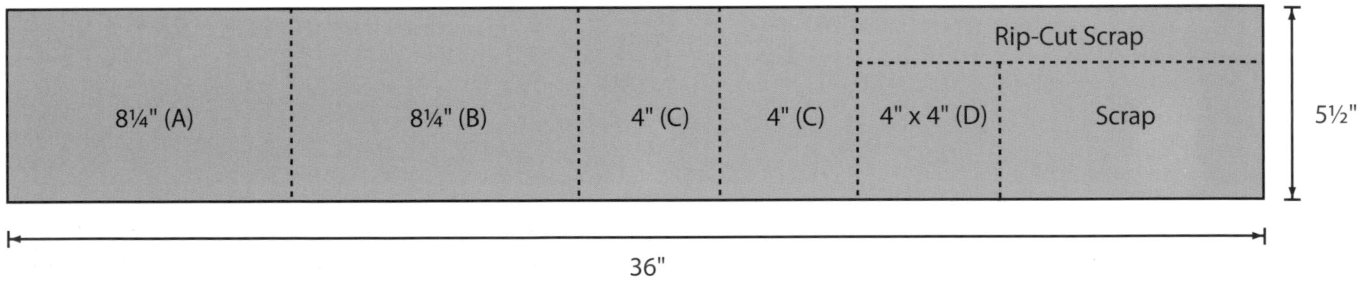

| 8¼" (A) | 8¼" (B) | 4" (C) | 4" (C) | 4" x 4" (D) | Rip-Cut Scrap |
| | | | | | Scrap |

5½"

36"

Starting with the Front

1 Lay out and cut the front (A) and back (B) from the 1 x 6 board. Use the diagram on page 42 as a guide.

2 Use Figure A to help you lay out the front (A) and back (B). On the front piece, be sure to mark the center points for where the 1¼-inch doorway and ⅜-inch perch should go.

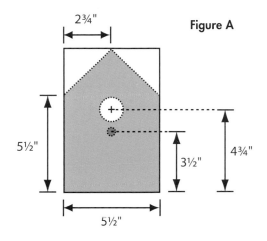

Figure A

Front (A)

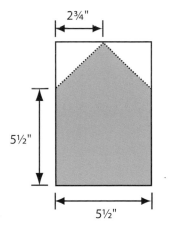

Back (B)

3 Use your saw to cut along the outside lines of the front (A) and back (B). Label both pieces and set the back aside.

4 Time to start drilling! Place the front (A) piece face up on your workbench with some scrap wood between the piece and the workbench. Then clamp the wood to the bench. Dimple the hole layout for the doorway. Chuck the 1¼-inch bit into your drill. Have your adult helper assist you with this step: carefully bore straight through the mark for the doorway.

5 Now for the perch hole. Flag the ⅜-inch bit to bore a ⅜-inch deep hole. Chuck the bit into the drill. Dimple the bore mark for the perch hole. Drill the hole straight into the mark. Have your adult helper remind you to stop drilling when the bottom of the flag reaches the surface of the front (A) piece. Set the piece aside.

Making the Sides

6 Cut the two sides (C) from the 1 x 6 board. Use the diagram on page 42 to help you.

7 You'll drill two more boreholes, using the ⅜-inch flag on the ⅜-inch bit again. These boreholes will hold the hanger (G) that lets you mount the birdhouse. Find one side (C) and set it face-up, with scrap wood under it, on your workbench. Transfer the layout marks for the ⅜-inch hole shown in Figure B onto the face.

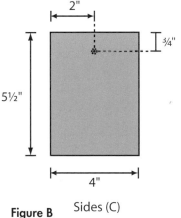

Figure B   Sides (C)

8 Clamp the wood. Dimple the hole layout. Drill the hole. Have your adult helper remind you to stop drilling when the bottom of the flag reaches the surface of the side (C) piece. Set the drilled piece aside. Repeat this step to bore a hole in the other side piece.

Making It Fit

9 The bottom (D) piece needs to be a square. To cut it to the correct width, you'll need to rip the remainder of your 1 x 6 board. Measure 4 inches from one edge of the board in two places. Mark that line and cut the piece. Discard the scrap wood (that's the piece measuring 1½ inches wide). Now cut the 4-inch wide board so that it is 4 inches long. Label the piece and set it aside.

10 Before you start nailing, it's important to make sure that all the pieces of your birdhouse fit together. Lay the bottom (D) face up. Place the front (A), back (B), and sides (C) around the bottom. Overlap their edges as shown in Figure C. Do they fit? Great! If not, use the rasp to shave off a bit of wood on the boards that don't fit. Set all the pieces aside except for the bottom and one side.

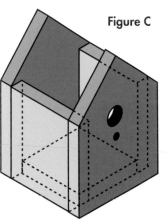

Figure C

Attaching the Sides

11 Line up the 4-inch edge of the side (C) with the bottom (D). Make sure the hole for the hanger (G) on your side piece is facing inside. Have your adult helper hold the pieces together tightly. Hammer two nails through the side into the edge of the bottom. Space the nails about 2½ inches apart.

12 Use your miter box to cut the hanger (G) and the perch (H). Label the pieces and set the perch aside.

13 Stick the hanger (G) into the hole in the side (C) you just nailed to the bottom (D). Line up the second side, sandwiching the hanger (G) between the two sides so that it fits into both holes.

Line up the bottom edge of the second side with the edge of the bottom. Pound two nails through the side into the edge of the bottom.

Attaching the Front and Back

14 Lay the assembly on its side, so that it makes a C when you look at it from above. Line up the front (A) so that it overlaps the edges of the bottom (D) and sides (C). Make sure the borehole you drilled for the perch (H) is facing up. Have your adult helper hold the front (A) in place while you drive six nails through it into the sides and bottom. Space the nails 1½ inches apart.

15 Flip the assembly and repeat step 14 to attach the back (B).

16 Put a few drops of glue on the end of the perch (H) and then set it firmly in the hole in the front (A).

Adding the Roof

17 Next, you'll cut out the short (E) and long (F) roof pieces from your 1 x 8 board.

18 To make the roof, ask your adult assistant to stand the short roof (E) on its end. Line up the end of the long roof (F) so that it overlaps the end of the short roof (see Figure D). Have your adult helper hold both boards in place while you drive two nails through the long roof into the end of the short roof. Space the nails about 3 inches apart.

19 The chain will go through the roof of the birdhouse. To make a hole for the chain, flip the roof and rest its peak on top of a piece of scrap wood. With your adult assistant holding the roof in place, mark a hole in the center on the joint, about 3⅝ inches from each end.

20 Drill a ⅜-inch hole through your mark on the roof. Hold the drill straight up and down so the bit comes out the peak of the roof.

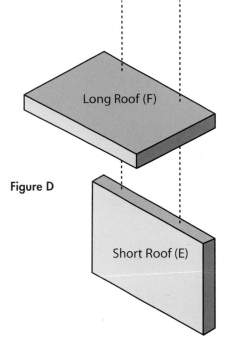

Long Roof (F)

Figure D

Short Roof (E)

Finishing Touches

21 Sand the birdhouse. Use a rasp to smooth out the entry hole. You don't want the birds to get splinters! Wipe off the sawdust and make sure everything is smooth.

22 Prime and paint the birdhouse. There are cow spots on the birdhouse in the photo on this page. To do this to your birdhouse, cover the primer with white paint, let it dry, and then add the black spots.

23 Thread the chain through the hole in the roof. You can use a piece of wire to fasten the chain to the hanger (G). Hang up your birdhouse outside and wait for your feathered visitors to move in!

Pooch Palace

Basic shapes are the building blocks for this awesome A-frame doghouse for small pooches.

SHOPPING LIST

- 2 x 4 x 4' softwood
- 2 x 2 x 24" softwood
- ¾" x 4' x 4' plywood sheet
- 3¼" or 3½" galvanized nails*
- 1½" galvanized nails
- 100-grit and 180-grit sandpaper
- Latex primer and paints
- Cushion

A galvanized nail has a special coating that keeps the nail from rusting. Check the label on the box.

TOOLS

- Layout tools
- Handsaw
- Compass tool
- Clamps
- Drill with ⅜" bit
- Jigsaw
- Hammer
- 1" paintbrush

EXPLODED VIEW

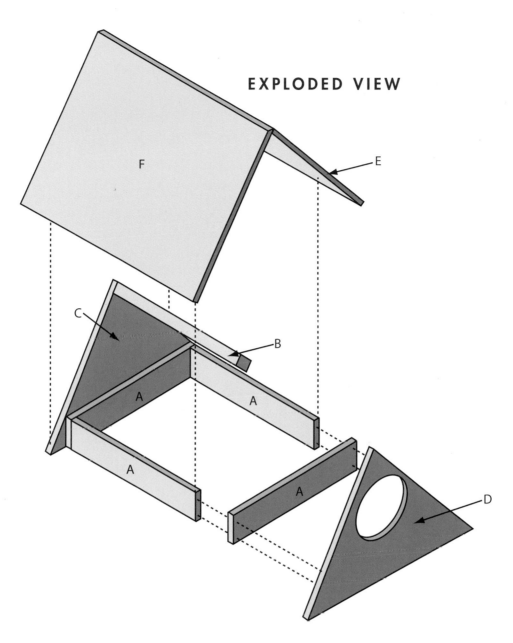

CUT LIST

Code	Part	Number	Size	Material
A	Base support	4	1½" x 3½" x 18"	Softwood
B	Roof support	1	1½" x 1½" x 18"	Softwood
C	Back	1	25½" x 23" x 23" triangle	Plywood
D	Front	1	25½" x 23" x 23" triangle	Plywood
E	Short roof	1	¾" x 24" x 23"	Plywood
F	Long roof	1	¾" x 24" x 24"	Plywood

4' x 4' Plywood

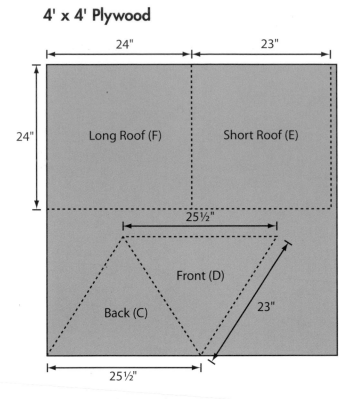

24"

24"

23"

24"

Long Roof (F)

Short Roof (E)

25½"

Front (D)

Back (C)

23"

25½"

Cutting the Plywood Pieces

1 Measure and mark the back (C), front (D), short roof (E), and long roof (F) pieces on the plywood sheet before you make any cuts. (Use the plywood diagram above as a guide.) Notice that the back and front pieces are the same size.

2 Cut out the pieces with your handsaw. Label them and set them aside.

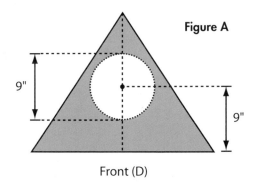

Figure A

9"

9"

Front (D)

Making an Entrance

3 Next, cut out the doorway so your pooch can get in and out of its house. Place the front (D) piece face-up on your workbench. Mark the center of the doorway (use Figure A as your guide). Draw the circle with your compass tool so that the diameter is 9 inches.

4 Place scrap wood between the front (D) piece and the workbench. Then clamp the wood. Chuck a ⅜-inch bit into your drill. Have your adult helper assist you with this step: Dimple and then bore a hole just inside the circle, anywhere on the circle.

5 Remove the scrap wood. Clamp the front (D) piece so that the entire circle you marked is hanging off the workbench.

6 **Ask your adult assistant for help when using the jigsaw.** Before turning it on, insert the first inch of the jigsaw's blade tip into the borehole. Line up the blade's teeth with the layout line.

7 To use the jigsaw, grip the handle, squeeze the trigger to turn it on, and move the saw forward slowly. As it cuts, turn the saw so the blade works along the curving layout line. Work at a controlled speed. If the blade goes off the line, release the trigger. (This turns off the saw.) Place the blade where you want it on the layout line and squeeze the trigger to begin cutting again. Midway through the cut, the scrap piece will need support. (Otherwise, it might tear away.) Use a length of scrap to support the waste piece from below. Keep all hands away from the jigsaw's blade. When your cut is finished, turn off the saw and unplug it. Then set the front (D) piece aside.

Building the Base

8 Now for the base of the doghouse. Cut the base supports (A). Label the pieces.

9 Attach two of the base supports (A) to each other. Set them on their edges. Line up the ends so the supports form an L shape. With your helper holding the pieces together, hammer two 3¼- or 3½-inch nails through the face of one support into the end of the other. Space the nails about 1½ inches apart.

10 Repeat step 9 to nail together the second pair of base supports (A).

11 Now you have two L-shaped pieces. Put them together, making a rectangle. Make sure the ends of the base supports (A) overlap as shown in Figure B. If they don't, they'll make a square. While your adult assistant holds the pieces firmly, hammer two 3¼- or 3½-inch nails through the face of one base support (A) into the end of the other. Repeat to nail together the other corner of the rectangle.

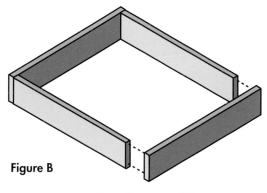

Figure B

Base Supports (A)

Adding the Front and Back

12 Ready to attach the front (D) and back (C) pieces to the base? Stand the back with its bottom edge touching the short side of the base. (It should be 18 inches long.) Hammer several 1½-inch nails through the back and into base. Space the nails about 3 inches apart.

13 Repeat step 12 to nail the front (D) to the opposite end of the base.

Attaching the Roof

14 Cut the roof support (B) piece and then label it.

15 The roof support (B) keeps the roof from falling in. You'll put it on before you add the roof. The ends of the roof support attach to the top corners of the back (C) and front (D). The face of the roof support is lined up with one of the angled edges of the front and back, so it's not centered. This is a bit tricky, so look at Figure C. Line up the roof support as shown and have your adult helper hold everything in place. Hammer two 1½-inch nails through the back into the end of the roof support. Nail two 1½-inch nails through the front into the other end of the roof support.

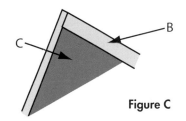

Figure C

16 Now you're ready to put on the roof. With the front of the doghouse facing you, line up the top edge of the short roof (E) with the top edge of the roof support (B) on the right side of the house. While your helper holds the short roof in place, measure where the short roof hangs over the front (D) and back (C). Adjust the roof so it hangs 2¼ inches beyond the front and back.

17 With your adult helper holding the short roof (E) in place, hammer several 1½-inch nails through its face into the roof support. Space the nails about 4 inches apart.

18 Nailing the short roof (E) to the front (D) and back (C) of the doghouse is a bit tricky. You can't see where the nails need to go because the roof covers the edges of the front and back pieces.

So, use your tape measure to mark a line on the face of the short roof, 2⅝ inches from the front edge. This line shows where the front piece is under the roof.

19 Now you can hammer nails through the short roof (E) into the edge of the front (D). Place the 1½-inch nails along the line you drew in step 18. Space the nails about 4 inches apart. If you pound in a nail and it doesn't hit the edge of the front, pull it out, move it, and try it again.

20 Repeat steps 18 and 19 to nail the short roof (E) into the edge of the back (C).

21 The last thing you do to finish attaching the short roof (E) is to nail it into the base. Because the roof is slanted, you'll need to mark where the corner of the base touches the short roof. Measure and mark a line on the short roof piece 3½ inches from the bottom. Hammer several 1½-inch nails through the short roof into the base. Space the nails 4 inches apart.

22 Repeat steps 16 through 21 to attach the long roof (F). The top of the long roof should be lined up with the top edge of short roof (E).

Finishing Touches

23 Sand the doghouse. Wipe off the sawdust. Prime and paint the doghouse.

24 Put a cushion inside the doghouse. If you put the doghouse outside, place it somewhere protected from rain and wind and put a piece of outdoor carpet beneath the cushion.

Squirrel Lounger

Squirrels need to kick back and relax sometimes, too.
Help them out by making this tiny easy chair.

SHOPPING LIST

- 1 x 6 x 36" softwood*
- 2 x 4 x 5" softwood
- 1½" finishing nails
- (3) No. 8 x 2" galvanized screws
- 100-grit and 180-grit sandpaper
- Latex primer and paints in your choice of colors
- Corncob

TOOLS

- Square
- Layout tools
- Handsaw
- Coping saw
- Clamps
- Hammer
- Drill and ⅛" drill bit
- Wood glue
- Rasp
- Screwdriver
- 1" paintbrush

** This is a great project to use small
pieces of wood from your scrap bin.*

EXPLODED VIEW

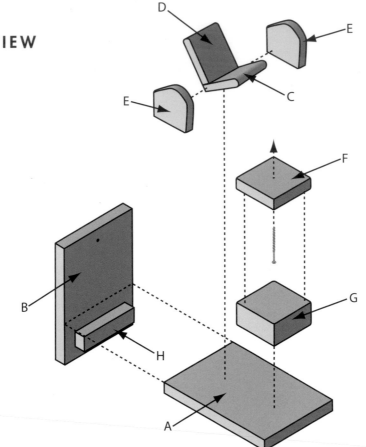

CUT LIST

Code	Part	Number	Size	Material
A	Base	1	¾" x 5½" x 8"	Softwood
B	Support	1	¾" x 5½" x 8"	Softwood
C	Chair seat	1	¾" x 3½" x 3"	Softwood
D	Chair back	1	¾" x 3½" x 3"	Softwood
E	Armrest	2	¾" x 3½" x 3"	Softwood
F	Cushion	1	¾" x 3" x 3"	Softwood
G	Footrest	1	1½" x 3" x 3"	Softwood
H	Brace	1	¾" x 1" x 4"	Softwood

1 x 6 Board

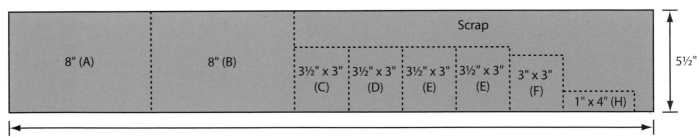

8" (A) 8" (B) Scrap 3½" x 3" (C) 3½" x 3" (D) 3½" x 3" (E) 3½" x 3" (E) 3" x 3" (F) 1" x 4" (H) 5½" 36"

Cutting the Parts

1 The most challenging part of this project is cutting out the pieces. You'll cut the easiest parts first. Lay out the 1 x 6 board as shown in the diagram on the opposite page. Cut out the base (A) and the support (B). Label the pieces.

2 The other pieces need a rip cut and a crosscut. Adjust the board and your clamp as you make each cut. Start with the rip cut for the chair seat (C), the chair back (D), and both armrests (E). Then crosscut the four pieces. Don't forget to label them.

3 Next, rip cut the top edge of the cushion (F). When you've finished, crosscut the piece and label it.

4 Finally, you'll cut out the brace (H). Use your saw to make a rip cut along the 4-inch edge, and then make the final crosscut.

5 The footrest (G) is cut from the 2 x 4 board. Lay out, cut, and label the piece. Set it aside for now.

Shaping the Armrests

6 Set the armrest (E) pieces flat on your workbench. Using the pattern on page 55, copy the illustration's curving line onto the face of one piece. Your line doesn't have to be exact.

7 Clamp the armrest (E) with the layout to the edge of your workbench. Use your coping saw to cut along the line.

8 Set the cut armrest (E) on top of the uncut one, aligning the square corners. Trace the shape you cut with your coping saw onto the bottom armrest. Then clamp the piece and cut along the line with your coping saw as you did with the first one. Set the pieces aside.

Rounding the Edges

9 To make your pieces look like real furniture, you'll use your rasp to round the edges a bit. Clamp the chair seat (C) to the edge of your workbench. Use the rasp to shape one of the 3-inch ends to resemble a rounded seat cushion on a chair.

10 Repeat step 9 to shape the short edge of the chair back (D). Now you have two cushions for the chair.

11 Finally, rasp all the edges of the armrests (E), the footrest (G), and the cushion (F).

12 Set the cushion (F) flat on your workbench. Slip a piece of scrap wood beneath it, and clamp the wood "sandwich" to the workbench. Draw two diagonals from corner to corner on the cushion's top face to find its center.

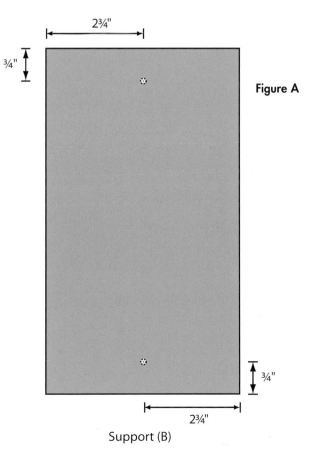

Figure A

Support (B)

13 Chuck your drill with a ⅛-inch bit. Dimple the center layout and bore a hole through it. Remove the clamp and set the cushion (F) aside.

14 Now clamp the support (B) piece to your worktable with scrap wood beneath it. This time, you'll lay out two holes. Each hole should be ¾ inch from an end and centered along the piece's middle (see Figure A). Dimple the layouts. Drill the holes and set the support aside.

Assembling the Ottoman

15 First you'll make the ottoman. Measure and mark a line ¾ inch from one end of the base (A). Run a thin circle of glue around the bottom face of the footrest (H). Press the footrest into place on the base, lining up its front edge with the line you just marked. Line up the side edges so they're both 1½ inches from the sides of the base.

16 With your adult assistant's help, flip the base (A) so it rests on the top of the footrest (H). Hammer two 1½-inch nails through the base and into the footrest. Put the nails in opposite corners. Flip the base right side up.

17 Now you're ready to attach the cushion (F). Drive a 2-inch screw through the pilot hole you made in step 13. Make the head of the screw even with the face of the cushion. You'll put the corncob on this spike later.

18 Flip the cushion (F) so the head of the screw is face up. Run a thin circle of glue around its face. Then, press the cushion onto the top of the footrest (G), with the pointy end of the screw sticking up. Line up the edges of the cushion with the edges of the footrest.

19 Drive two nails through the corners of the cushion (F) and into the footrest (G). Make sure you put these nails in corners opposite from the nails you hammered through the base (A) into the footrest in step 16.

Building the Chair

20 Stand the chair back (D) on its rounded end. Run a thin line of glue along the flat end. Lay the unrounded end of the chair seat (C) face on the end of the chair back to form an L shape. Line up the edges and hammer two nails through the face of the chair seat and into the end of the chair back.

21 Now you'll attach the armrests (E) to the chair. Lay the chair on its side, so it rests on one edge of the chair back (D) and seat (C). Place the inside face of the first armrest on top of the chair. Tilt the armrest so it sits on the chair as shown

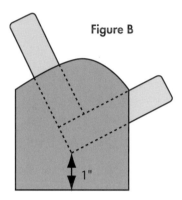

Figure B

1"

in Figure B. The chair joint should be about 1 inch from the flat bottom edge of the armrest. Hammer a nail through the face of the armrest into the edge of the chair back. Hammer another nail through the armrest and into the edge of the chair seat.

22 Flip the chair so it rests on the face of the armrest (E) you just attached. Place the inside face of the second armrest on top of the chair. Line it up with the first armrest. Then use your square to make sure the flat bottoms of the armrests are perfectly even. (They have to be even to attach the chair to the base.) Hammer two nails through the armrest into the chair, as you did in step 21.

23 It's time to put the chair in place. Measure and mark a line 1¼ inches from the back of the footrest (G). Set the chair on the base with the front edge of the armrests (E) touching the line you just marked. Flip the base (A) so it rests on the chair and footrest, being careful that the two pieces don't jiggle as you flip them. While your adult helper holds the pieces together, hammer a nail through the bottom face of the base and into one armrest. Hammer another nail through the base into the other armrest. If the nail doesn't go into the armrest, pull it out, move it, and try again.

Adding the Support

24 First, you'll attach the brace (H) to the support (B). Lay the support face up. Measure and mark a line 1 inch from one end.

25 Run a thin line of glue along the edge of the brace (H). Put it in place, so its bottom edge is touching the 1-inch line. Line up the edges of the brace and the support (B).

26 Carefully flip the support (B) so it rests on the base. Hammer two nails through the support's back face and into the brace (H). Space the nails 2 inches apart.

27 Now you'll attach the base (A) to the support (B). Ask your adult helper to stand the base on its front end. Place the support on top of the base, lining up the base's bottom face with the top of the brace (H). While your adult helper holds everything together, hammer two nails through the face of the support and into the base. These nails should be about 2 inches apart.

Finishing Touches

28 Sand the squirrel lounger.

29 Next, prime and paint it.

30 To mount the squirrel lounger, have your adult assistant help you position it on a tree or post at least 5 feet off the ground. Drive two screws through the pilot holes in the support (B) into the tree.

31 Carefully screw or twist the end of a corncob onto the screw in the footrest. Wait for your neighborhood squirrels to settle in for a snack.

CHAIR PATTERN

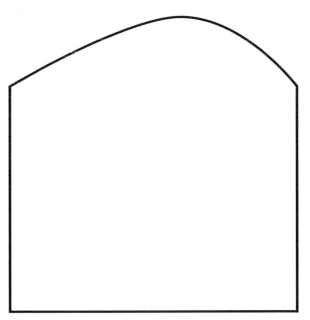

Bird Buffet

This project will provide a feast for your feathered friends.

SHOPPING LIST

- 1 x 8 softwood, at least 10" long
- 1 x 10 softwood, at least 12" long
- ¾" x 1½" x 12" craft lumber
- ½" x 1½" x 36" craft lumber
- 17-gauge x 1" brads
- 1½" finishing nails
- (2) ³⁄₁₆" x 3" screw hooks
- #200 twist chain, at least 4' long
- 100-grit and 180-grit sandpaper
- Latex paint and primer
- Bird seed

TOOLS

- Layout tools
- Clamps
- Handsaw
- Miter box
- Hammer
- Drill with ³⁄₁₆" bit
- Screwdriver
- 1" paintbrush

EXPLODED VIEW

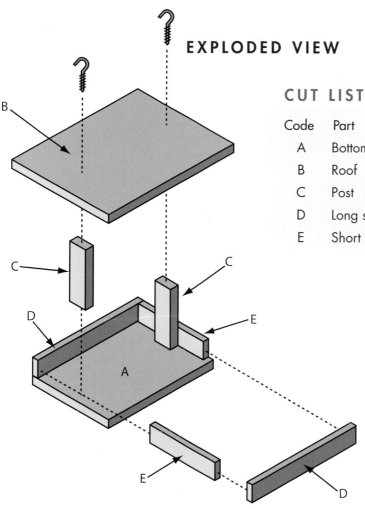

CUT LIST

Code	Part	Number	Size	Material
A	Bottom	1	¾" x 7¼" x 10"	Softwood
B	Roof	1	¾" x 9¼" x 12"	Softwood
C	Post	2	¾" x 1½" x 5"	Softwood
D	Long side	2	½" x 1½" x 10"	Softwood
E	Short side	2	½" x 1½" x 6¼"	Softwood

Cutting out the Pieces

1 Lay out, cut, and label the bottom (A) piece from the 1 x 8 board. Set it aside.

2 On the 1 x 10 board, lay out and cut the roof (B) to length. Label it and set it aside.

3 Measure and mark the length of both posts (C) on the ¾ x 1½-inch board. Clamp the board and cut out the pieces. Label them and set them aside.

4 Now for the sides. Lay the ½ x 1½-inch board on your workbench. Lay out both long sides (D). Clamp the board and cut out the pieces. Label them and set them aside.

5 Using the same board, lay out and cut the short sides (E). Don't forget to label them.

6 You'll start building your Bird Buffet by nailing together the long sides (D) and the short sides (E) to form a box. Ask your adult helper to stand a short side on end. Lay the face of one long side on top of it, making an L shape. Hammer two brads through the face of the long side and into the end of the short side. Space the brads about ½ inch apart (see Figure A). Set the L-shaped piece aside.

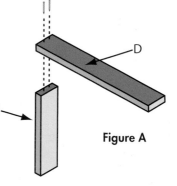

Figure A

7 Repeat step 6 to put together the other long (D) and short sides (E).

8 Now you'll nail the two L-shaped pieces together to make a box. Set the first L-shaped piece on its long side, with the short side (E) sticking up. Put the second L-shaped piece on top, so they form a box with the second long side (D) overlapping the short side. With your adult assistant holding the pieces together, hammer two brads through the face of the long side and into the end of the short side. Space the brads about ½ inch apart.

9 Flip the box and nail the last joint together with two brads as you did in step 8.

Attaching the Bottom

10 To add the bottom (A) to the box, rest the box on the edges of the long (D) and short (E) sides. Set the bottom on the box, lining up its edges with the sides.

11 Hammer several nails through the bottom (A) and into the edges of the sides. The nails should be about ¼ inch from the edge and about 3 inches apart.

Adding the Posts

12 Now you'll attach the posts (C) to the box. To mark where they will go, flip the box so that it rests on its bottom (A). On one short side (E), draw two diagonal lines on its face from opposite corners. They'll intersect in the center of the face.

13 Repeat step 12 to mark the center of the opposite short side (E).

14 Set the first post (C) face up on the workbench. Measure and mark the center of the post (¾ inch from each edge) near the end.

15 Set your square on the end of the post (C), and mark a line lengthwise (from end to end) through the center of the post.

16 Repeat steps 14 and 15 to mark the other post (C).

17 Have your adult assistant help you attach the posts (C) to the box. Set the first post inside the box, lining up its centerline with the mark you made in the center of the short side (E). Make sure the end of the post is flat against the bottom (A).

18 With your adult assistant holding the post in place, hammer a brad through the face of the short side (E) and into the face of the post (C). Is the post at a right angle to the bottom? Use your square to check. If it's not, wiggle it or tap on it gently with your hammer until it is. Then hammer another brad through the side and into the post.

19 Repeat steps 17 and 18 to attach the other post to the other side of the box.

Adding the Roof

20 Now you're ready to add the roof (B). Lay the roof face up. Measure and mark the center point of the short edges on both ends. Use your square to connect the center points so that a line runs through the center of the roof from end to end.

21 Set the box on your workbench. Put the roof on top of the posts (C). Line up the centerline on the roof (B) with the centerlines on the posts.

22 Measure how far the ends of the roof (B) overhang the posts (C). Is it the same distance? Great! If not, adjust the position until the same amount of roof overhangs each post.

23 While your adult assistant holds everything together, hammer two nails through the roof (B) and into the end of the first post (C). These nails should go into opposite corners of the post.

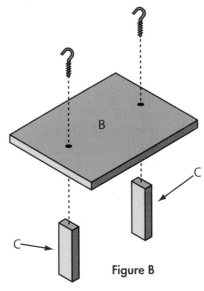

Figure B

24 Repeat step 23 to attach the roof (B) to the other post (C).

25 To hang the Bird Buffet, you'll need to put two screw hooks in the roof (B). (Both ends of the chain will attach to the hooks.) The screw hooks need to go through the roof into the center of the posts (C). Use your layout tools and Figure B to mark the roof where the center of each post is.

26 Dimple the marks you made in step 25. Flag a ³⁄₁₆-inch bit to bore a ¼-inch hole. Chuck the bit into your drill and bore a hole through each mark, stopping when the bottom of the flag touches the wood.

27 Insert a screw hook into one of the pilot holes and twist it clockwise with your fingers to drive the screw into the wood. If it's too hard to turn, put the end of your screwdriver through the hook and twist it.

28 Repeat step 27 to put the other screw hook in the roof (B).

Finishing Touches

29 Sand the Bird Buffet. Wipe off the sawdust.

30 Prime and paint the Bird Buffet.

31 Decide where you want to hang it. Thread one end of the chain through a screw hook. Do the same on the other side.

32 Hang the Bird Buffet. Fill it with birdseed and keep an eye out for your first customers!

Cat Tail Cat Toy

Your cat will flip for this rope toy. And your parents will be relieved that the kitty has something to scratch besides the furniture.

SHOPPING LIST

- 1 x 4 x 6' softwood
- 1¼" dowel, at least 25" long
- ¾" sisal or other natural rope, at least 48" long*
- 1¼" finishing nails
- No. 6 x 1¼" screws
- (1) No. 8 x 2" screw
- 100-grit and 180-grit sandpaper
- Large electrical staples*
- Latex primer and paints
- * Ask for help finding this at the lumberyard.

TOOLS

- Layout tools
- Handsaw
- Miter box
- Hammer
- Drill with ¹⁄₁₆" and 1¼" bits
- Screwdriver
- 1" paintbrush
- Scissors

CUT LIST

Code	Part	Number	Size	Material
A	Top	1	¾" x 3½" x 24"	Softwood
B	Bottom	1	¾" x 3½" x 24"	Softwood
C	Leg	2	¾" x 3½" x 3½"	Softwood
D	Post	1	1¼" x 24"	Dowel

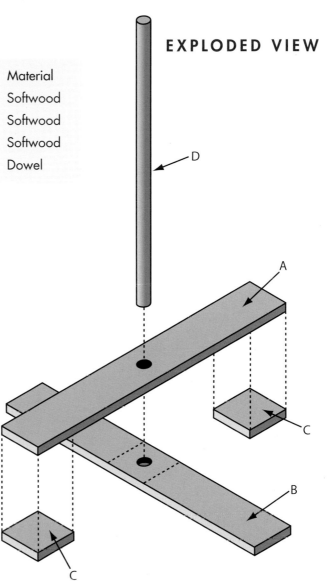

Cutting the Parts

1 Lay the 1 x 4 board on your workbench. Measure and mark the length of the top (A) and then crosscut it with your handsaw. Label the piece and set it aside.

2 Repeat step 1 to cut the bottom (B) and both legs (C).

3 Lay the 1¼-inch dowel in your miter box. Measure and mark the length of the post (D). Hold the dowel firmly against the miter box and cut the line you marked. Set it aside.

Building the Base

4 Put the top (A) face up on your workbench. Set one leg (C) on the end of the top, lining up the ends and edges as shown in Figure A.

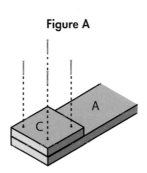

Figure A

5 With your adult helper holding the pieces together, hammer four nails through the leg (C) and into the top (A). Set a nail in each corner, about ½ inch from the edge.

6 Repeat steps 4 and 5 to attach the second leg (C) to the other end of the top (A).

7 Flip the top (A) so that it stands on the legs (C). Transfer the layout marks in Figure B onto the face of the top. The 1¼-inch hole goes in the center to hold the post (D). The four pilot holes are where the screws will attach the top to the bottom (B).

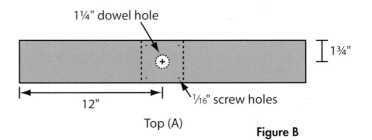

1¼" dowel hole

1¾"

12"

1/16" screw holes

Top (A)

Figure B

8 Set the top (A) on the bottom (B), forming a cross shape. Center the top along the length of the bottom. Make sure the pieces are square.

9 Chuck the 1/16-inch bit into your drill, clamp the top (A), and dimple the pilot-hole layouts. Bore the four holes. Use the screwdriver to drive four screws through the pilot holes and into the bottom (B). You now have a base for your cat toy.

Attaching the Post

10 Chuck the 1¼-inch bit into your drill. Flag the bit to drill a hole that's 1¼ inches deep. While your adult assistant holds the top (A) and bottom (B) tightly together, drill a hole where you marked in step 7. Bore through the top and partway into the bottom. Stop drilling when the bottom of the flag touches the face of the top. Only the tip of the spade bit should go all the way through the bottom.

11 Now you're ready to attach the post (D) to the base. Turn the base upside down. Have your adult assistant stand the post on one end. Fit the post into the 1¼-inch hole in the base.

12 Chuck a 1/16-inch bit into your drill. While your adult assistant holds the base and the post (D) tightly together, drill a hole through the bottom (B) and into the end of the post. Use the small hole made by the tip of the 1¼-inch bit in the bottom as your starting point.

13 Drive a 2-inch screw through the pilot hole you just made and into the post (D). This will hold the post securely to the base.

Finishing Touches

14 Sand all the parts of the cat toy. Wipe off the sawdust.

15 Prime the cat toy.

16 Paint the cat toy, starting with the base. It's easiest to paint the post (D) last. Remember to use two coats of paint, letting the paint dry between coats.

17 When the paint is completely dry, set the cat toy on your workbench. It's time to attach the rope. With your adult assistant's help, use the hammer to pound a large staple through the end of the rope and into the bottom of the post (D). Make sure the rope is tightly attached to the post. (Use another staple if you want.)

18 Tightly wind the rope around the post (D). Have your adult assistant help you keep each turn of the rope tight against the one below it.

19 When you get to the top of the post (D), attach the rope to the post with another staple. Two staples are even better!

20 Trim the end of the rope neatly with scissors, so that the rope hangs a few inches below the base. Separate the strands of the rope's end if you want.

21 Put your cat toy out for your kitty and let the fun begin!

Observation Station

Observe critters up close with this catch-and-release nature project.

SHOPPING LIST

- 2 x 2 x 8' softwood
- (2) 2 x 2 x 6' softwood
- No. 8 x 2" galvanized screws
- ¼" x 36" x 48" galvanized mesh hardware cloth
- Craft wire, at least 50" long
- 100-grit and 180-grit sandpaper
- Exterior-grade wood sealer

TOOLS

- Layout tools
- Miter box
- Handsaw
- Clamps
- Drill with ⅛" drill bit
- Screwdriver
- Wood glue
- Felt-tip pen
- Tin snips
- Staple gun with ¼" staples
- 2" paintbrush

CUT LIST

Code	Part	Number	Size	Material
A	Long rail	4	1½" x 1½" x 18"	Softwood
B	Short rail	4	1½" x 1½" x 15"	Softwood
C	Stile	4	1½" x 1½" x 15"	Softwood
D	Mesh square	5	15½" x 15½"	Hardware cloth

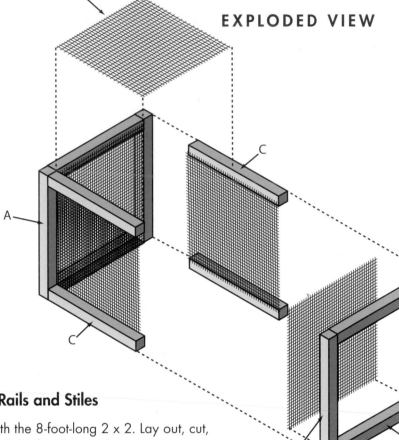

EXPLODED VIEW

Cutting the Rails and Stiles

1 Start with the 8-foot-long 2 x 2. Lay out, cut, and label the four long rails (A). Use your miter box for these cuts.

2 Repeat step 1 to lay out and cut the short rails (B) and the stiles (C) from the two 6-foot-long 2 x 2 boards. Use your miter box and label the pieces. Then set them aside.

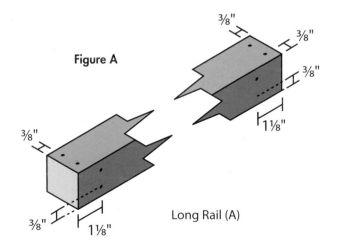

Figure A

⅜"   ⅜"

⅜"

1⅛"

⅜"

⅜"   1⅛"

Long Rail (A)

3 Set a long rail (A) flat on your workbench. Figure A shows how each long rail has a total of eight pilot holes. On two side-by-side faces, you'll mark a pair of holes near either end. On one face, each pilot hole will be ⅜ inch from the end and the edge. On the other face, each hole will be 1⅛ inches from the end and ⅜ inch from the edge. Lay out the pilot holes for all four long rails.

4 Ask your adult assistant for help with this step. Set a piece of scrap wood under a long rail (A) and clamp the board "sandwich" to your workbench. With a ⅛-inch bit chucked in your drill, bore the four pilot-hole marks on one face of the rail. Do your best to drill straight through the board at each mark. Flip the board a quarter turn so that the other four marks are face up, and drill through the four marks.

5 Repeat step 4 to drill the pilot holes for the other three long rails (A).

Making Squares

6 The Observation Station is made out of squares. You'll start by assembling two of them. Then you'll connect the squares to form a box.

7 Set one long rail (A) and one short rail (B) in front of you. Line up the end of the short rail with the face of the long rail, making an L shape. Make sure the pilot holes ³⁄₈ inch from the end of the long rail are aligned with the end of the short rail (see Figure B). The pilot holes that are 1 ¹⁄₈ inches from the end of the long rail should be face up.

Figure B

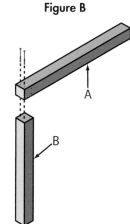

A

B

8 While your adult assistant holds the pieces together, drive a screw through one of the pilot holes in the long rail (A) and into the end of the short rail (B). Drive another screw into the second pilot hole. Now you have an L shape.

9 Repeat steps 7 and 8 with another long rail (A) and short rail (B).

10 Now you'll make a square out of the two L-shaped pieces. Line them up so the ends of the short rails (B) are inside the long rails (A). The pilot holes in the ends of the long rails should be lined up with the ends of the short rails. Drive a screw through each pilot hole in the long rails and into the ends of the short rails. Look—it's a square! Set it aside.

11 Repeat steps 7 through 10 with the other two long rails (A) and short rails (B), making a second square.

Connecting the Squares

12 The stiles (C) will attach to each corner of the squares to build a box. You'll drive a screw through the pilot holes 1 ¹⁄₈ inches from the end of the long rails (A) into the ends of the stiles.

13 Lay the first stile (C) on your workbench. Have your adult helper hold one of the squares on its side. Line up the corner of the square with the end of the stile. Make sure the pilot holes are positioned so that you can drive screws through them and into the end of the stile. While your helper holds the pieces in place, drive a screw through each pilot hole in the long rail (A) and into the end of the stile.

14 Repeat step 13 to attach the three other stiles (C) to the first square.

15 Flip the assembly so that it rests on the square you just attached. Line up the second square on the ends of the stiles (C) and drive a screw through each pilot hole in the long rails (A) and into the ends of the stiles. Congratulations! You've made the box.

Attaching the Mesh Squares

16 Lay the hardware cloth on your workbench. You may need to flatten it with a scrap board. Use your layout tools and a felt-tip pen to mark five 15½ x 15½-inch squares on the metal cloth.

17 Cut the squares along the layout lines with your tin snips. Be careful because the metal cloth is very sharp! Ask your adult assistant for some help if you need it.

18 Look at Figure C to see how each corner of the five squares is snipped out. This allows the squares to fit neatly into the inside corners of the box you've built. Cut the corners from each square with your tin snips. It's best to test-fit one square corner before you cut the other three, just to be sure it will fit well. If not, remove a bit more metal from the corner.

19 It's time to put the mesh squares (D) on the box. You'll use a staple gun to shoot the staples into the wood, sandwiching the mesh in place. Set the box on your workbench with the squares on the top and bottom. With your adult assistant's help, fit the first mesh square inside the first side of the box. The sides of the square will overlap the stiles (C).

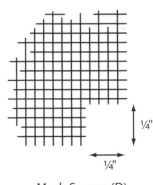

Mesh Square (D)

Figure C

20 Put on your safety glasses. Look at your staple gun. The staples come out of the slot in the bottom. Line up the slot so it's on top of the mesh and the wood. Press the gun tightly against the wood and squeeze the trigger. Use plenty of staples, attaching the cloth squares (D) securely to the wood.

21 Repeat steps 19 and 20 to attach three more mesh squares (D) to the other three sides of the box. The one left over will go on top.

Adding the Top

22 Attaching the top mesh square (D) is a bit tricky because there's no more room left to staple the square to the wood. So you'll weave the craft wire between the top edges of the four other cloth squares to the edges of the top piece.

23 Flip the box so that it's standing upside down. Place the last mesh square (D) on top of the box. Slide the square inside the box, so it rests against the top. (Remember, the top is resting on the workbench because the box is upside down.)

24 Thread a length of craft wire through the holes in the mesh on one edge of the top piece. Then go through the holes in the top edges of

TIP

If a staple doesn't go all the way into the wood, use your hammer to pound it the rest of the way in.

the mesh on the adjacent side, weaving the top and side together. Wrap the wire around the mesh to secure the ends. Cut the wire when you've finished.

25 Repeat step 24 to finish attaching the top mesh square (D) to the remaining three sides.

Finishing Touches

26 Sand the Observation Station and wipe off the sawdust.

27 Paint two coats of the exterior-grade sealer onto the Observation Station.

28 Set it up outside. Leave it on the ground for a few hours. Then look closely inside. Do you see any insects in there? Be patient—they're shy! Release them after an hour or two.

Quintuple Bike Stand

You don't have to wrestle with a tangled pile of bikes anymore. Five rides fit in this easy-to-build rack.

SHOPPING LIST

- (3) 2 x 4 x 6' softwood
- (2) 2 x 2 x 8' softwood
- ¾" x 24" x 48" plywood
- 3¼" galvanized nails
- 2½" galvanized nails
- 100-grit and 180-grit sandpaper
- Exterior-grade wood sealer

TOOLS

- Layout tools
- Handsaw
- Miter box
- Clamps
- Hammer
- Drill with ⅛" bit
- 2" paintbrush

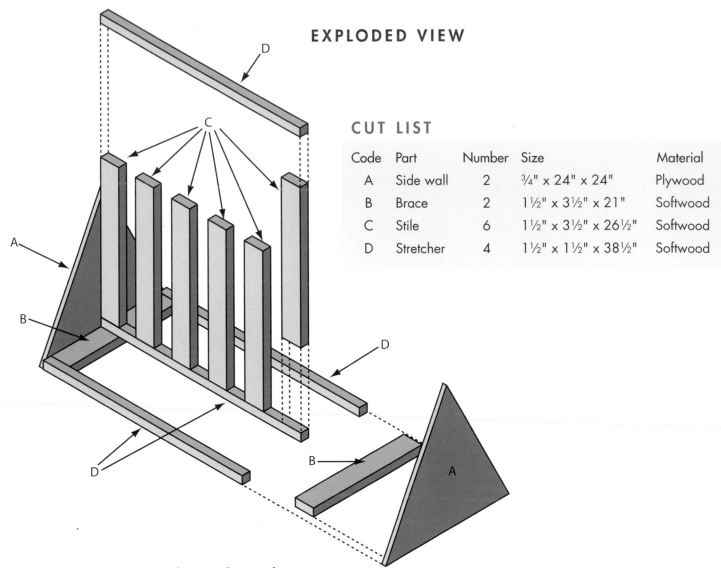

EXPLODED VIEW

CUT LIST

Code	Part	Number	Size	Material
A	Side wall	2	¾" x 24" x 24"	Plywood
B	Brace	2	1½" x 3½" x 21"	Softwood
C	Stile	6	1½" x 3½" x 26½"	Softwood
D	Stretcher	4	1½" x 1½" x 38½"	Softwood

Cutting the Braces, Stiles, and Stretchers

1 Lay out and cut the braces (B) and stiles (C) to length from the three 2 x 4 boards. Label the pieces and set them aside.

2 From the two 2 x 2 boards, lay out the lengths for the stretchers (D). Use the miter box to crosscut the pieces. Don't forget to label them.

3 Only two of the four stretchers (D) will have pilot holes for nails. Transfer the 12 pilot-hole marks in Figure A onto each of the two stretchers.

4 Clamp one of the marked stretchers (D) to your workbench so a pilot hole hangs over the edge. Dimple the hole layouts. Chuck the ⅛-inch bit into your drill. Then have your adult assistant help you with this step: Carefully bore straight through one mark. Adjust the piece and repeat to drill all of the pilot holes.

5 Repeat step 4 to drill all of the pilot holes in the second stretcher (D) piece. Set both pieces aside.

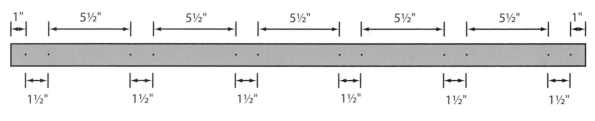

Figure A   Stretcher (D) Pilot Holes

6 Because the pieces you're working with are so large, you may need to do the next few steps on the floor. First, you'll attach the stiles (C) to two of the stretchers (D) to make the middle part of the bike stand. The stretchers you'll use for the next few steps are the two with pilot holes.

7 Lay the first stretcher (D) face up. Set the first stile (C) face up with its end touching the bottom edge of the stretcher at one end. The two pieces will form a corner. While your adult assistant holds the pieces together, hammer two 3¼-inch nails through the pilot holes in the edge of the stretcher and into the end of the stile.

8 Repeat steps 6 and 7 to line up and nail a second stile (C) to the other end of the stretcher (D), forming a corner at the opposite end.

9 Lay the second stretcher (D) against the bottoms of the stiles (C). Hammer two 3¼-inch nails through the pilot holes in the stretcher and into the ends of the stiles. You've just made a rectangle.

10 Attach the four remaining stiles (C) between the stretchers (D), spacing them equally between the attached stiles. The stiles should be about 3½ inches apart. Set the middle part of your bike stand aside.

2' x 4' Plywood

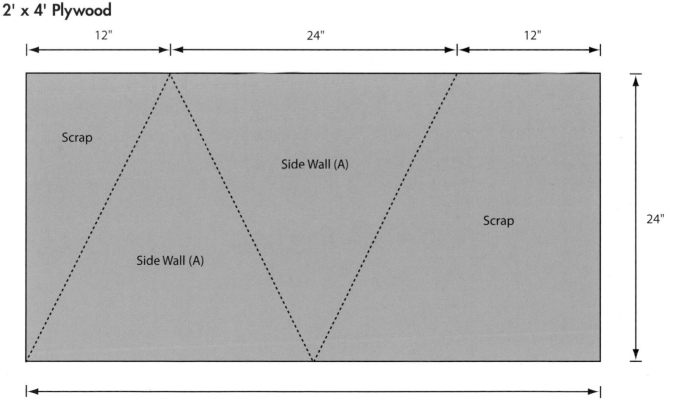

Quintuple Bike Stand

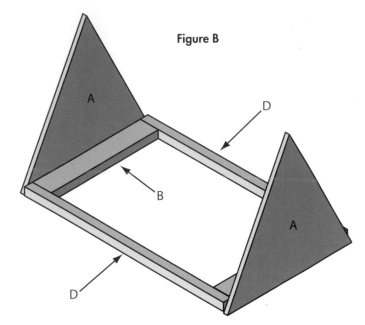

Figure B

A

D

B

A

D

Building the Ends

11 Measure and mark the two side walls (A) on the plywood. (Use the diagram on page 69 as your guide to draw the two triangles.)

12 Clamp the plywood to your workbench and cut out the pieces. Label the side walls (A).

13 Now you'll attach the braces (B) to the side walls (A) of the bike stand. Lay the first brace on its edge. Have your adult helper hold the first side wall on top of the brace. Line up the 24-inch side of the triangle with the face of the brace. Center the brace between the corners of the side wall. The side wall should overhang the ends of the brace by 1½ inches on either side. Hammer a row of 2½-inch nails through the face of the side wall and into the edge of the brace. Space the nails about 2 inches apart.

14 Repeat step 13 to attach the other brace (B) to the other side wall (A).

15 Now you'll attach the stretchers (D) that don't have any holes drilled in them to the side walls (A). Stand the side walls on the floor (the braces will balance them). Line up the side walls so the braces (B) are on the inside, facing each other. Lay the two stretchers on the floor between the side walls (see Figure B). The ends of each stretcher should connect with the side walls at the outside corner, forming a rectangle. One edge of each stretcher will be pressed against a brace.

16 With your adult helper holding the parts together, hammer two 2½-inch nails through a side wall (A) into the stretcher (D).

17 Repeat step 16 on the other three corners of the side walls (A), nailing both of the stretchers (D) in place.

18 The last step is to attach the middle part of the bike stand to the side walls (A). Have your adult assistant hold the middle part between the side walls. The bottom should rest on top of the braces (B). Use your layout tools to make sure the stand is centered between the side walls and is straight up and down.

19 With your adult helper holding the pieces tightly together, drive a row of 2½-inch nails through the first side wall and into the edge of the stile. The nails should be spaced about 6 inches apart. Repeat this step to attach the other end.

Finishing Touches

20 Sand all the parts of the bike stand. Wipe off the sawdust.

21 Seal your project with two coats of clear exterior-grade wood sealer, letting each coat dry completely.

22 Your bike stand will last for many years if you keep it in a sheltered place such as under a carport or in your garage. Now get rolling!

Paddle Racer

Make two or more of these wind-up speedboats and turn them loose in your swimming pool. See which one wins the race!

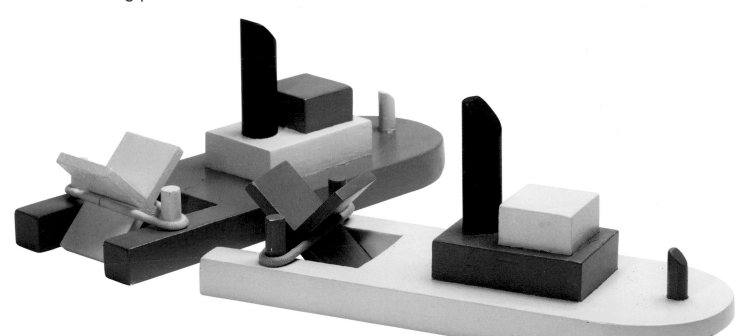

SHOPPING LIST

- 1 x 4 x 18" softwood
- ¼" x 1½" x 12" craft lumber
- ¾" x 6" dowel
- ⅜" x 6" dowel
- Rubber band or elastic hair tie
- 1½" finishing nails
- (1) No. 8 x 1½" screw
- 100-grit and 180-grit sandpaper
- Latex primer and paints

TOOLS

- Layout tools
- Compass
- Clamps
- Coping saw
- Handsaw
- Miter box
- Drill with ⅛" and ⅜" bits
- Rasp
- Screwdriver
- Wood glue
- 1" paintbrush

EXPLODED VIEW

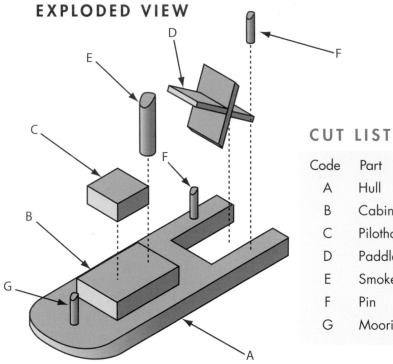

CUT LIST

Code	Part	Number	Size	Material
A	Hull	1	¾" x 3½" x 10"	Softwood
B	Cabin	1	¾" x 2" x 3"	Softwood
C	Pilothouse	1	¾" x 1½" x 1½"	Softwood
D	Paddle	2	¼" x 1½" x 2¾"	Craft lumber
E	Smokestack	1	¾" x 2"	Dowel
F	Pin	2	⅜" x 1"	Dowel
G	Mooring post	1	⅜" x 1"	Dowel

1 x 4 Board

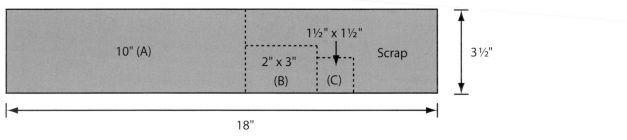

Cutting the Hull

1 Square the end of the 1 x 4 board. Starting from the squared end, lay out the length of the hull (A).

2 Using Figure A as a guide, lay out the three lines for the cutout where the paddles will go on the hull (A). Then, at the other end of the piece, use your compass to make the rounded layout for the front of the boat.

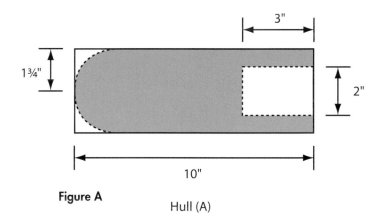

Figure A

Hull (A)

3 Clamp the board so that the rounded layout line hangs over the edge of the workbench. Use your coping saw to cut along the line.

4 Adjust the board so that the opposite end hangs over the workbench edge. With the coping saw, remove the paddle cutout you marked. Label the hull (A) and set it aside.

Cutting the Cabin and Pilothouse Pieces

5 Set the rest of the 1 x 4 board back on your workbench. Use the diagram on the opposite page to help you lay out the cabin (B) and pilothouse (C) pieces.

6 You'll need to rip cut the cabin (B) piece first to get it to the proper width. Then use your handsaw to make the crosscut. Label the cabin and set it aside.

7 Repeat step 6 to rip and crosscut the pilothouse (C). Label it and set it aside.

Cutting out the Paddles

8 Set the ¼-inch craft lumber on your workbench. Lay out two paddles (D) so that the layouts are spaced at least 1 inch apart on the board (see Figure B). Also lay out the notches in each paddle. (The paddles will fit together in the notches.) The open end of each notch should be lined up with a long edge of your board.

9 Clamp the craft lumber to your workbench. First, use your coping saw to remove the notches from each paddle (D). Then cut out the two paddles. Label them and set the pieces aside.

Cutting the Dowels

10 Set the ¾-inch dowel on your workbench. Measure and mark 2 inches from one end. Set the dowel against the miter-box fence and cut it to length. Label this as your smokestack (E) piece and set it aside.

11 Set your ⅜-inch dowel on your workbench. Repeat step 10 to lay out and cut three 1-inch lengths. Label two of the pieces as pins (F) and the other as the mooring post (G). Set the pieces aside. (You can put your saws away, too!)

Drilling Pilot Holes

12 Set the hull (A) flat on your workbench. Lay out the two pilot holes for the pins (F) and the hole for the mooring post (G) as shown in Figure C.

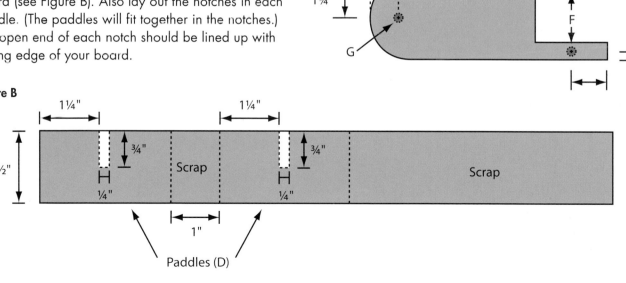

Figure C

Figure B

Paddles (D)

73

13 Dimple the hole layouts. Chuck a ⅜-inch bit into your drill and flag it for a depth of ¼ inch. Bore the three holes to the flagged depth. Set the hull (A) aside.

14 Set the cabin (B) flat on your workbench. Lay out the pilot-hole mark shown in Figure D.

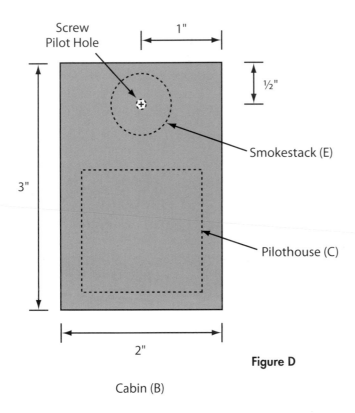

Figure D

Cabin (B)

15 Dimple the hole layout. Chuck the ⅛-inch bit into your drill and bore through it.

Rasping Your Parts

16 Use your rasp to shape the ends of the smokestack (E) and mooring post (G) to 45-degree angles (see Figure E).

17 Flip your hull (A) upside down and round the front end of its bottom face with your

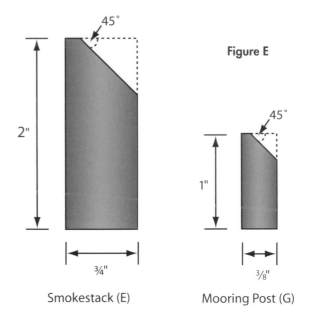

Figure E

Smokestack (E)   Mooring Post (G)

rasp. If you keep the curve smooth and even, your boat will steer straight and true. See Figure F.

Putting It All Together

18 First you'll attach the smokestack (E) to the cabin (B). Ask your adult helper to stand the smokestack on end. Put the cabin on top, lining up the center of the smokestack with the pilot hole in the cabin. Drive a screw through the cabin and into the smokestack.

19 Set the cabin (B) on its bottom, with the smokestack (E) sticking up. Run several lines of wood glue along the face of the pilothouse (C). Press the pilothouse into place on the cabin in front of the smokestack, ¼ inch from the front edge and ¼ inch from each side. Then set the cabin assembly aside to dry.

TIP

Drill "on" not "into" your workbench! A piece of scrap wood set between your workbench and the project piece you're working on will help protect your workbench surface from damage.

Figure F

Rounded
Front

Hull (A)

20 Now you'll put the paddle (D) pieces together. Sand the notches you made in steps 8 and 9. Then fit the paddles together, sliding their notches into each other. Do they fit? Great! If not, sand out a little more of the wood until they do. Take the paddle pieces apart and add a drop of glue to the inside edge of one notch. Slide the paddle pieces together again. Let the paddles dry.

21 Set the hull (A) face up, with the pilot holes facing you. Put a bit of glue on the flat end of the mooring post (G). Stick it into the pilot hole at the front of the hull. Make sure it stands straight up and down.

22 Put some glue on the end of the first pin (F). Insert it in the pilot hole next to the paddle cutout at the back end of the hull (A). Make sure the pin is straight up and down.

23 Repeat step 22 to put the second pin (F) in place.

24 Last building step! It's time to glue the cabin (B) into place. Run a few lines of glue along the bottom of the cabin (where the screw head is). Press it into place on the hull (A) 2¾ inches from the front and ¾ inch in from each side.

Finishing Touches

25 Sand the Paddle Racer. Wipe off all the sawdust. Prime and paint the Paddle Racer.

26 Now you'll attach the paddles (D) to the pins (F) with the rubber band. Stretch the rubber band over the ends of both pins, sandwiching the paddle in between. Who knew building a boat was this easy?

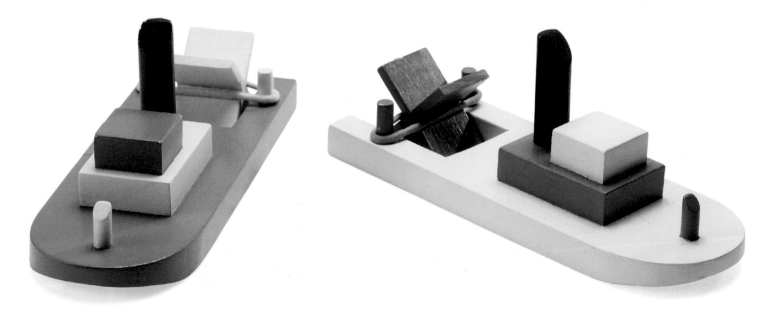

Rope Ladder

Have a tree house or just want to climb?
This ladder will take you to higher places!

SHOPPING LIST

- (2) 2 x 4 x 6' softwood
- 100-grit and 180-grit sandpaper
- Latex primer and paints
- ½" braided polypropylene rope, about 16' long for the six-step ladder*

* *If you want to add more steps, add 3'
   of rope for each extra step*

TOOLS

- Layout tools
- Handsaw
- Clamps
- Drill with ⅝" bit
- Rasp
- 1" paintbrush
- Scissors

EXPLODED VIEW

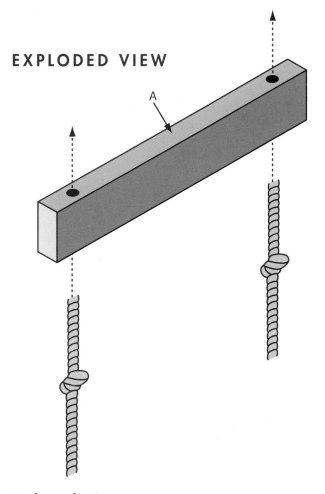

A

Figure A

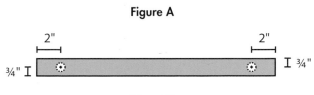

2"   2"

¾" I ⫿ ⚙   ⚙ ⫿ I ¾"

Step (A)

That's the other borehole for this piece. Repeat on the opposite edge. (You'll have matching marks and lines on each edge.) Set this piece aside.

3 Repeat step 2 for all six steps (A). Set them aside. Take a break!

4 Clamp one of the marked steps (A) so that a borehole hangs over the edge of the workbench. Dimple the hole layout. Chuck the ⅝-inch bit into your drill. Have your adult assistant help you with this step: Carefully drill straight into the mark. Only drill halfway through the step. Adjust the piece and repeat to drill the borehole on the opposite end—only halfway through.

5 Then flip the step (A), clamp it, and drill through both borehole layouts—all the way through the step. (This is the best way to drill through wide boards.) The bit may "grab" a little when it reaches the halfway point; just keep it steady. Set the step aside.

6 Repeat steps 4 and 5 to drill all of the boreholes holes in the steps (A).

Sanding the Steps

7 Sand each step (A). Use the rasp to sand the boreholes. Wipe off the sawdust.

8 Prime and paint the steps (A).

Making the Steps

1 Lay out and cut the steps (A) to length from the 2 x 4 boards. Label the pieces and set them aside.

2 Using Figure A as your guide, lay out the boreholes on the edges of each step (A). To do this, you'll mark a squared line 2 inches from each end. (Remember to work on the edges of the pieces.) Measure and mark a spot on that line ¾ inch from the edge of the face. This is one borehole location. Repeat on the opposite end of the edge.

CUT LIST

Code	Part	Number	Size	Material
A	Step	6	1½" x 3½" x 20"	Softwood

Tying the Knots

9 Now you'll attach the rope. Cut two equal lengths of rope. You'll need two ropes that are 8 feet long for a six-step ladder.

10 Wrap masking tape around the cut ends of rope. This will keep the ends from fraying.

11 Thread the end of the first length of rope through one of boreholes in the first step (A). Slide the step along the rope so that it rests 18 inches from the end of it. Tie a knot below the step.

12 Repeat step 11, threading the second length of rope through the other side of the step (A).

13 Add the next step (A), 12 inches below the first. Tie knots below the step.

14 Repeat step 13 until you've added all the steps (A).

15 With your adult assistant's help, tie the top of the rope ladder to a sturdy branch or to your tree house. Start climbing! Make sure the ground beneath your swing is soft or well-covered in mulch—just in case you fall off the ladder.

Speed Board

Everybody needs a set of wheels. Keep it for yourself or build this scooter for your younger sibling.

SHOPPING LIST

- 1 x 8 softwood, at least 26" long
- 1 x 6 x 6' softwood
- 1 x 4 softwood, at least 20" long
- 2 x 4 softwood, at least 6" long
- 1" dowel, at least 10" long
- (1) pair of skateboard trucks with wheels and hardware*
- No. 8 x 1½" screws
- 1½-inch finishing nails
- 100-grit and 180-grit sandpaper
- Latex primer and paints

* Available at a local skate shop or online. You can also reuse an old set or find them at a garage sale.

TOOLS

- Layout tools
- Compass
- Clamps
- Coping saw
- Hammer
- Drill with ⅛" and 1" drill bits
- Miter box
- Handsaw
- Wood glue
- Screwdriver
- Wrenches (for the bolts that come with your wheel hardware)
- 1" or 1½" paintbrush

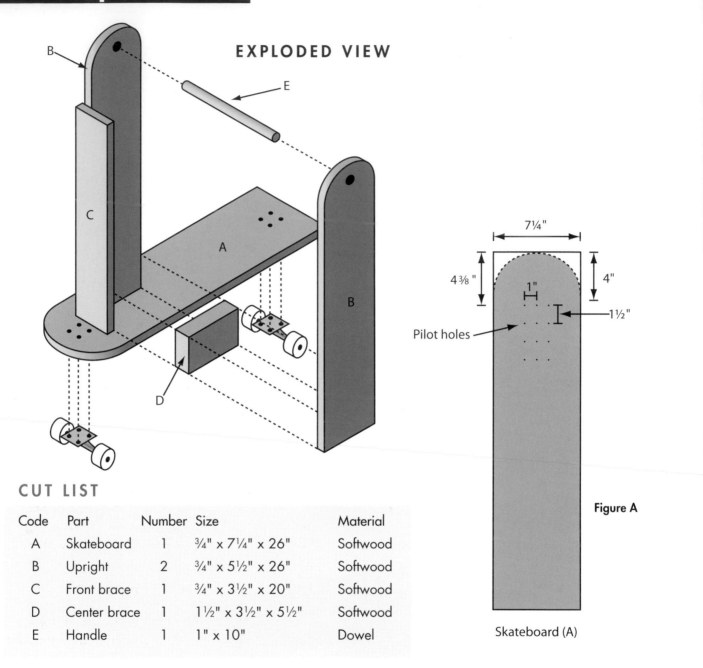

EXPLODED VIEW

7¼"

4⅜"

1"

4"

1½"

Pilot holes

Figure A

Skateboard (A)

CUT LIST

Code	Part	Number	Size	Material
A	Skateboard	1	¾" x 7¼" x 26"	Softwood
B	Upright	2	¾" x 5½" x 26"	Softwood
C	Front brace	1	¾" x 3½" x 20"	Softwood
D	Center brace	1	1½" x 3½" x 5½"	Softwood
E	Handle	1	1" x 10"	Dowel

Building a Skateboard

1 Lay the 1 x 8 board flat on your workbench. Square the end of the board and lay out the length of the skateboard (A).

2 Draw the rounded layout at the marked end of the skateboard (A) with your compass (see Figure A). Use the 4-inch hole on your compass.

3 Clamp the skateboard (A) so that the rounded layout line hangs over the edge of the workbench. Use your coping saw to cut along the line. Label the piece.

Drilling Pilot Holes

4 The Speed Board's pieces are secured with screws to make this project extra tough. With the skateboard (A) flat on your workbench, mark the layouts for the pilot holes on the board's face. Figure A shows you exactly where to mark it.

5 Set one of the board's layouts on your workbench so that it overhangs the edge. Clamp the board. Dimple the hole layouts. With a ⅛-inch bit chucked in your drill, bore the pilot holes. Repeat to bore the rest of the marks in the skateboard.

Rolling It Out

6 Time for the wheels! Place the wheel trucks 2 inches from each end of the skateboard (A). If the front truck is in the way of pilot holes you made in steps 4 and 5, move it closer to the front of the board.

7 Mark the placement of the pilot holes (where you'll put the bolts to attach the trucks).

8 Have your adult assistant help you with this step. Clamp the skateboard (A) to your workbench. Dimple the pilot-hole layouts. Choose a drill bit that is the same width as the bolts you'll use to attach the trucks. Chuck the bit into the drill and drill the holes.

9 Flip the skateboard (A) right side up. Insert the bolts through the pilot holes and tighten them with wrenches (and a screwdriver, depending on the type of bolt) to attach the trucks to the bottom of the skateboard.

Rounding off the Uprights

10 Set the 1 x 6 board flat on your workbench. Lay out and then cut the two uprights (B) to length.

11 Like the skateboard (A), the uprights (B) also each have one square end and one rounded end. Using Figure B as a guide, mark the rounded edge of each upright with the 3-inch hole on your compass.

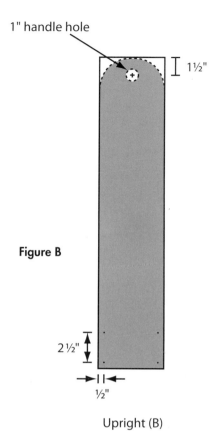

1" handle hole

1½"

Figure B

2½"

½"

Upright (B)

12 Clamp an upright (B) to your workbench, leaving the rounded layout line hanging over the edge. Cut along the line with your coping saw. Label the piece. Repeat this step for the other upright (B).

Cutting the Other Handle Pieces

13 Lay the 1 x 4 board flat on your workbench. Lay out, cut, and then label the front brace (C).

14 Next, lay out and cut the center brace (D) from the 2 x 4 board. Label it.

15 Lay out the length of the handle (E) on the dowel. Set the dowel against the miter-box fence. Cut the layout with your handsaw. Label the handle. Set your saws aside, too!

Drilling the Handle Holes

16 Lay an upright (B) flat on your workbench. Look at Figure B to lay out the 1-inch pilot hole for the dowel handle. Slip a piece of scrap wood beneath the upright, and clamp the "sandwich" to your workbench. Dimple the pilot-hole layout.

17 With a 1-inch bit chucked in your drill, bore a hole through the upright (B). Repeat to lay out, clamp, dimple, and drill the second upright. Your adult assistant can help you with the drill if needed.

Drilling Holes for Screws

18 With an upright (B) flat on your workbench, mark the layouts for the four screw pilot holes on the board's face. Figure B shows exactly where to mark it. Lay out the second upright, too.

19 Clamp one of the uprights (B) to your workbench so that the pilot-hole layouts hang over the edge. Dimple the pilot-hole layouts. With a ⅛-inch bit chucked in your drill, bore the pilot holes.

20 Repeat step 19 to drill the pilot holes for the second upright (B).

21 Using Figure C as your guide, repeat steps 18 and 19 to lay out and drill the pilot holes in the face of the front brace (C).

Assembling the Handle Stand

22 Ask your adult helper to hold one of the uprights (B) on top of the center brace (D) so that the face of the center brace aligns with the bottom end of the upright's

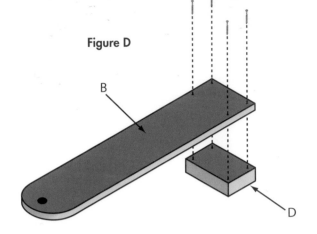

Figure D

B

D

face (see Figure D). The four pilot holes in the upright should be centered directly over the face of the center brace.

23 Drive a screw through the pilot hole in the upright (B) and into the face of the center brace (C). Drive the other three screws through the pilot holes.

24 Flip the upright (B) and center brace (C) so that it rests on the face of upright. Line up the second upright with the face of the center brace as you did in step 22. Drive screws through each of the pilot holes.

25 Stand the handle assembly on end. Slide the handle (E) through the pilot holes in the uprights (B). Center the handle and hammer a nail into the top edge of each upright and through the dowel.

Putting It All Together

26 Flip the skateboard (A) upside down. Ask your adult assistant to hold the bottom of the handle stand against the top of the skateboard, lined up with the pilot holes. Drive screws through the bottom of the skateboard, into the end of the stand.

Finishing Touches

27 Sand the Speed Board. Wipe off the sawdust. Prime and paint it.

28 Take it out for a test drive! Make sure the rider wears a helmet.

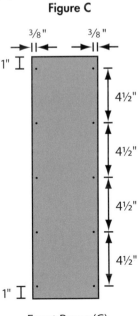

Figure C

3/8"   3/8"

1"

4½"

4½"

4½"

4½"

1"

Front Brace (C)

Estimated Time: 4 to 6 hours

Balance Beam

Can you and your friends "walk the plank?"

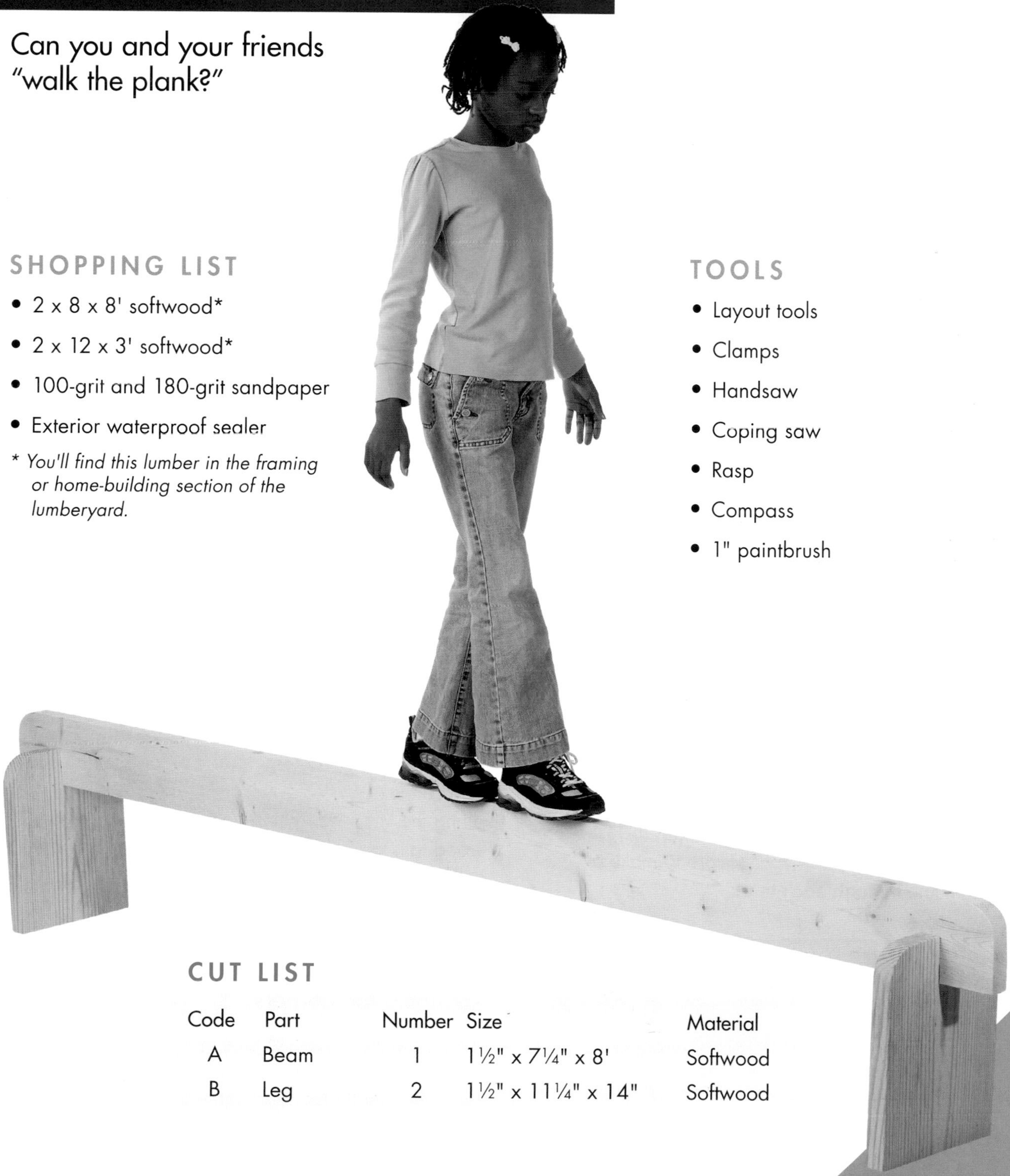

SHOPPING LIST

- 2 x 8 x 8' softwood*
- 2 x 12 x 3' softwood*
- 100-grit and 180-grit sandpaper
- Exterior waterproof sealer

** You'll find this lumber in the framing or home-building section of the lumberyard.*

TOOLS

- Layout tools
- Clamps
- Handsaw
- Coping saw
- Rasp
- Compass
- 1" paintbrush

CUT LIST

Code	Part	Number	Size	Material
A	Beam	1	1½" x 7¼" x 8'	Softwood
B	Leg	2	1½" x 11¼" x 14"	Softwood

Estimated Time: 3 to 4 hours

Baseball Hold-All

This is way more than a shelf! A long slot, shallow holes, and short pegs store bats, balls, and gloves perfectly. (It will work for softball equipment, too.)

SHOPPING LIST

- 1 x 4 x 4' softwood
- $\frac{3}{8}$" x 12" dowel
- $1\frac{1}{2}$" finishing nails
- 100-grit and 180-grit sandpaper
- Latex primer and paints
- (2) Screws*
- (2) Screw anchors (optional)

TOOLS

- Layout tools
- Handsaw
- Clamps
- Hammer
- Drill with $\frac{1}{8}$", $\frac{3}{8}$", and $1\frac{1}{4}$" bits
- Coping saw
- Miter box
- Wood glue
- Rasp
- 1" paintbrush
- Screwdriver

* Ask for help at your hardware store or lumberyard to select the right screws to hang the Baseball Hold-All on your wall. Take this book with you (steps 17 to 20 describe one way to fasten the screws).

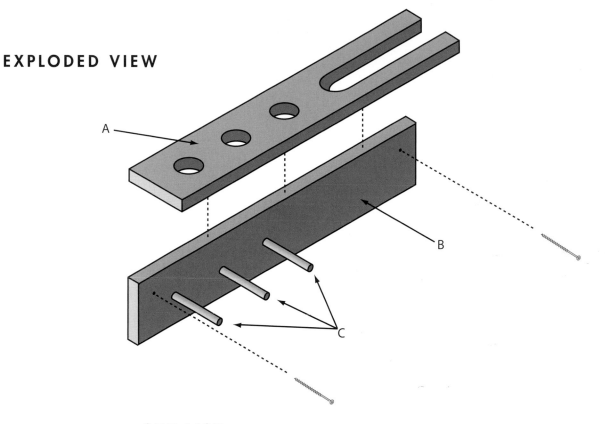

A

B

C

CUT LIST

Code	Part	Number	Size	Material
A	Top	1	¾" x 3½" x 18"	Softwood
B	Support	1	¾" x 3½" x 18"	Softwood
C	Peg	3	⅜" x 3"	Dowel

Making the Top

1. Lay out and cut the top piece (A) to length. Don't forget to label it.

Figure A

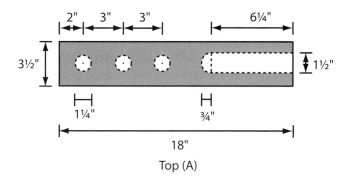

Top (A)

2. Transfer the layout marks shown in Figure A onto the face of the top (A). Notice that there are three holes and one slot to draw. The holes will hold baseballs; the slot is for bats.

3. First you'll drill the holes. Place the top (A) face up on your workbench, slide a piece of scrap beneath it, and clamp it all in place. Dimple the layouts for the baseball holes. Chuck the 1¼-inch bit into your drill. (This is a large bit that is difficult for anyone to handle, so you must have your adult helper assist you with holding the drill.) Carefully bore straight through one of your marks. If the bit

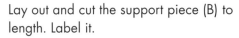

gets stuck, stop drilling, raise the bit slightly, and begin again. Repeat to drill the other holes in the top.

4 Now for the slot. Adjust the top piece (A) so the layout mark for the slot hangs over the edge of your workbench. Clamp the board in place. Use your handsaw to make the two long parallel cuts in the bat-slot layout. Stop cutting just before you reach the curved part of the layout.

5 Finish cutting the curved part of the cut line with your coping saw.

Building the Support

6 Lay out and cut the support piece (B) to length. Label it.

7 Transfer the layout marks shown in Figure B onto the face of the support (B). Notice that there are five holes to mark on the support. The three ⅜-inch holes will hold pegs for your gloves. You'll use the two ⅛-inch pilot holes for the screws that mount the project to the wall.

Figure B

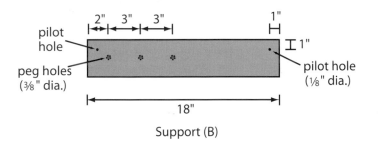

Support (B)

8 Begin with the ⅛-inch pilot holes. Place the support (B) face-up on your workbench, slide a piece of scrap beneath it, and clamp the board in place. Dimple the hole layouts. Chuck the ⅛-inch bit into your drill. Carefully bore straight through one mark. Repeat for the other ⅛-inch pilot hole.

9 Make sure there's scrap under the three remaining holes in the support (B). Dimple those holes. Find your ⅜-inch bit and flag it at ½ inch. Chuck the flagged ⅜-inch bit into your drill, and drill each of the holes ½ inch deep. (You can ask your adult helper to remind you to stop drilling when the bottom of the flag touches the surface of the piece.)

10 Now for the pegs (C). Use your miter box to cut the dowel into three 3-inch pieces. Label the pieces and set them aside.

Assembling the Shelf

11 First you'll attach the support (B) to the top (A). Have your adult helper stand the support on its edge. Lay the top over it, lining up the ends and edges. Make sure the holes for the pegs (C) are beneath the overhang of the top.

12 While your adult helper holds the pieces together, hammer three nails through the face of the top (A) and into the edge of the support (B). The nails should be about ⅜ inch from the edge of the top and spaced about 5 inches apart.

13 Now you'll insert the pegs (C). Lay the shelf down so it's resting on the back face of the support (B). The ⅜-inch boreholes should be face up. Put a drop or two of glue on the end of the first peg and set the glued end in a ⅜-inch hole. You may need to use your hammer to tap the dowel all the way into the hole. Wipe up any drippy glue with a damp paper towel.

14 Repeat step 13 to glue the other two pegs (C) into the holes. Now, tilt all three pegs up slightly so they point toward the top (A). (This will keep your gloves from slipping off the pegs.) Make sure the pegs are lined up with each other, and then let the glue dry.

Finishing Touches

15 Use the rasp to smooth out the curved end of the bat slot and inside the holes that will hold the balls.

16 Sand the Baseball Hold-All. Wipe off the sawdust. Then prime and paint it.

17 When the paint is completely dry, fasten your project to the wall. Get your adult helper to find two studs in the wall. (The 16-inch spacing between the pilot holes should be the right distance for hitting the center of two studs. If it's not, use screw anchors to support the Hold-All.)

18 Hold the Baseball Hold-All against the wall so that it's level on the top (A) and the right height for you to reach. (Remember, it will have bats hanging in the bat slot!) Stick your pencil through the pilot hole, marking the spot on the wall where the screw will go.

19 Take the Baseball Hold-All off the wall. Chuck the 1/8-inch bit into the drill. Then, drill a hole into the wall where you marked. Have your adult helper hold the Baseball Hold-All against the wall again. Use a screwdriver to drive a screw through the pilot hole in the Baseball Hold-All and into the pilot hole in the stud.

20 Step back and look at the Baseball Hold-All while your adult helper holds it. Does it look level? Great! If not, move the end that hasn't been screwed to the wall up or down. When it's level, repeat steps 18 and 19 to install the second screw. Play ball!

Favorite Things Shelf

Display your keepsakes in this easy, multi-shelf unit.
Lay or hang it on any side for just the right fit and look.

SHOPPING LIST

- (2) 1 x 4 x 6' hardwood*

- 1¼" finishing nails

- 100-grit and 180-grit sandpaper

- Latex stain and polyurethane varnish

- 4½" x 3" flat corner braces with screws**

* If you want to stain your display shelf like this one, use a hardwood like oak. If you'd rather paint your project, use a softwood.

**Use these special pieces of hardware to make your display shelf sturdier. Ask for help finding them at the lumberyard or hardware store.

TOOLS

- Layout tools

- Handsaw

- Hammer

- Rasp

- Cotton rags

- 1" paintbrush

- Drill with ¹⁄₁₆" bit

- Screwdriver

EXPLODED VIEW

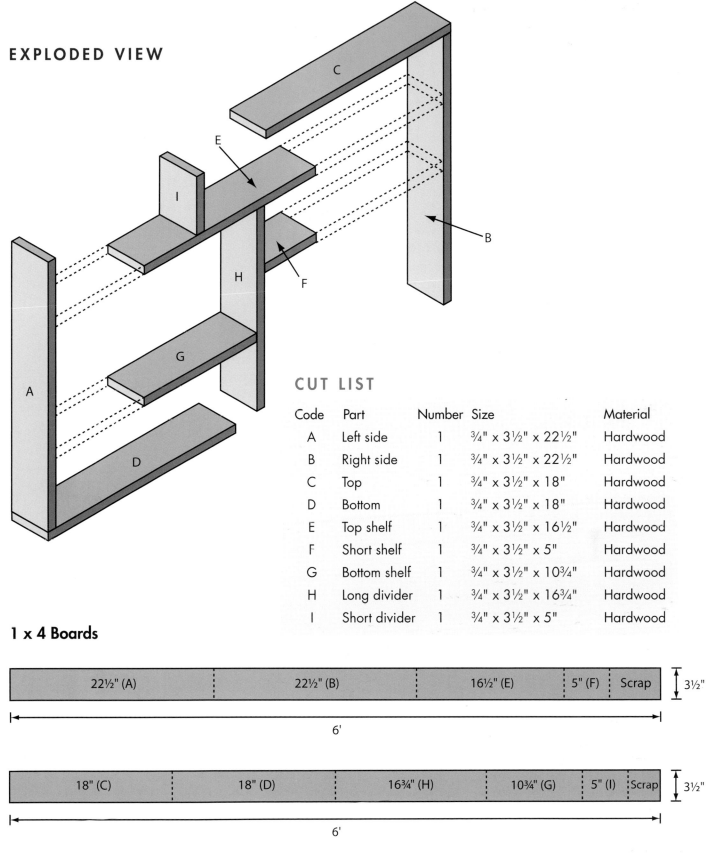

CUT LIST

Code	Part	Number	Size	Material
A	Left side	1	¾" x 3½" x 22½"	Hardwood
B	Right side	1	¾" x 3½" x 22½"	Hardwood
C	Top	1	¾" x 3½" x 18"	Hardwood
D	Bottom	1	¾" x 3½" x 18"	Hardwood
E	Top shelf	1	¾" x 3½" x 16½"	Hardwood
F	Short shelf	1	¾" x 3½" x 5"	Hardwood
G	Bottom shelf	1	¾" x 3½" x 10¾"	Hardwood
H	Long divider	1	¾" x 3½" x 16¾"	Hardwood
I	Short divider	1	¾" x 3½" x 5"	Hardwood

1 x 4 Boards

22½" (A)	22½" (B)	16½" (E)	5" (F)	Scrap

3½"

6'

18" (C)	18" (D)	16¾" (H)	10¾" (G)	5" (I)	Scrap

3½"

6'

Cutting the Pieces

1 Lay out and cut all of the pieces. Use the two diagrams of the 1 x 4 boards on page 91 to help you. Be sure to square both ends of each piece; all of the pieces need to fit together perfectly to create this shelf. And label those pieces—there are a lot of them!

Building the Box

2 You'll start by transferring the layout lines in Figure A to the left side (A), right side (B), top (C), and bottom (D). On the sides, be sure to label the "top" and "bottom" ends. On the top and bottom, label the "left" and "right" sides.

3 Now it's time to make a simple box. Ask your adult assistant to stand the left side (A) on end so the bottom is touching the floor. Lay the left side of the top (C) on the end of the side, lining up the edges. Hammer two finishing nails through the face of the top into the end of the left side. Put the nails about 2 inches apart. Now you have an L shape.

4 Repeat step 3 to attach the right side (B) to the right end of the bottom (D), making another L-shaped piece.

5 To finish making the box, fit the L-shaped pieces together, matching the corners of the sides (A & B), top (C), and bottom (D). Ask your adult assistant to hold the pieces while you hammer two nails through the face of the top and into the end of the right side (B). Space the nails about 2 inches apart.

6 Flip the box so it rests on the top (C), and then repeat step 5 to nail the bottom (D) to the left side (B).

Inserting the Shelves

7 The shelves and the dividers go in next. Rest the box on the edges of the sides (A & B), top (C), and bottom (D). Use the exploded view on page 91 to help you set the shelves and dividers in the box. Do the pieces fit? Great! If a piece is too long, use your rasp to remove wood until it fits or cut another piece a bit shorter. If a piece is too short, cut a new piece and try it again.

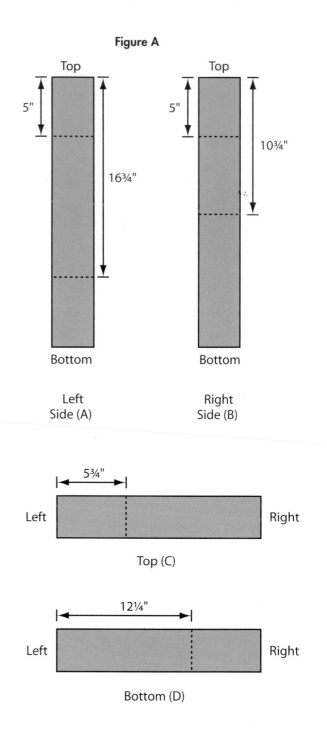

Figure A

Top — 5" — 16¾" — Bottom
Left Side (A)

Top — 5" — 10¾" — Bottom
Right Side (B)

Left — 5¾" — Right
Top (C)

Left — 12¼" — Right
Bottom (D)

8 First you'll attach the top shelf (E). Align the top face of the top shelf with the top layout marks on the left (A) and right (B) sides (5 inches below the top). See Figure B. While your adult assistant holds the pieces in place, hammer two nails through the face of one side and into the end of the top shelf. Space the nails about 2 inches apart. Hammer two nails through the face of the other side and into the other end of the top shelf.

10 With your adult assistant holding the pieces together, hammer two nails through the face of the bottom (D) into the end of the long divider (H). Space the nails 2 inches apart. Hammer two nails through the face of the top shelf (E) into the other end of the long divider.

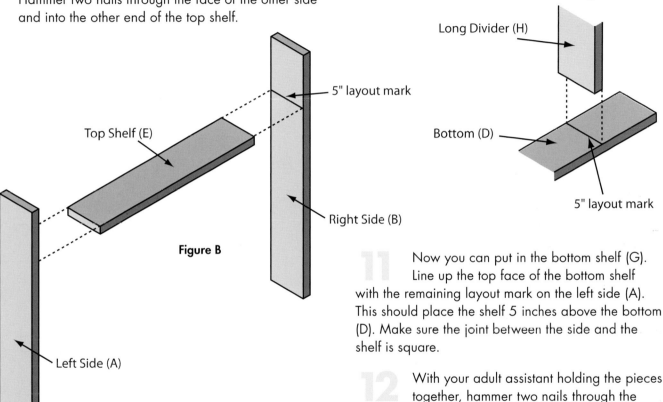

Figure B

5" layout mark

Top Shelf (E)

Right Side (B)

Left Side (A)

Figure C

Long Divider (H)

Bottom (D)

5" layout mark

9 Next you'll attach the long divider (H). Line up the right face of the long divider with the layout mark on the bottom (D), 5 inches in from the right. See Figure C. Use your square to make sure the divider is straight up and down.

11 Now you can put in the bottom shelf (G). Line up the top face of the bottom shelf with the remaining layout mark on the left side (A). This should place the shelf 5 inches above the bottom (D). Make sure the joint between the side and the shelf is square.

12 With your adult assistant holding the pieces together, hammer two nails through the face of the left side (A) into the end of the bottom shelf (G). Space the nails 2 inches apart. Hammer two nails through the face of the long divider (H) into the other end of the bottom shelf.

13 Now for the short pieces. Start with the short shelf (F). Line up the top face of the shelf with the top layout mark on the right side (B). Make sure the joint is square.

14 With your adult assistant holding the pieces together, hammer two nails through the face of the right side (B) into the end of the short shelf

(F). Space the nails 2 inches apart. Hammer two nails through the face of the long divider (H) into the other end of the short shelf.

15 It's time to put in the last piece! Line up the left face of the short divider (I) with the layout mark on the top (C), 5¾ inches from the left side (A). Make sure the joint is square.

16 With your adult assistant holding the pieces together, hammer two nails through the face of the top (C) into the end of the short divider (I). Space the nails 2 inches apart. Hammer two nails through the face of the top shelf (E) into the other end of the short divider.

TIP

Nailing pieces together when you don't have quite enough room to swing your hammer can be tricky! To make this easier, hold the nail at a slight angle. (Not so much that it will pop through the face of the piece you're nailing into though!) Then you can swing your hammer at an angle to hit the nail, which gives you a little more room.

Sanding and Varnishing

17 Sand all parts of the Favorite Things Shelf. Wipe off the sawdust.

18 To stain the shelf unit, use a clean cotton rag to wipe stain onto all of its parts. Don't apply the stain so thickly that it gets drippy or puddles up on the project. Let the stain dry completely.

19 Paint two coats of varnish onto the Favorite Things Shelf, letting the first coat dry before applying the second. This will seal the wood.

Adding the Corner Braces

20 Lay the shelf unit face-down on top of newspaper or cloth. Line up a corner brace on the edge of a corner where the left side (A) joins the top (C). Center the brace on the corner. Use your pencil to mark where the screws will go through the bracket into the edge of the side and top.

21 Flag a ¹⁄₁₆-inch bit to drill a ½-inch deep pilot. Dimple each mark. Chuck the bit into your drill. With your adult assistant holding the shelf unit firmly, drill a pilot hole through each mark. Drive a screw through each pilot hole in the brace.

22 Repeat steps 20 and 21 to put a corner brace in each corner of the shelf unit. Now put your favorite things on it!

Jewelry Tree

Go out on a limb and make this artistic project. The curvy branches are a perfect fit for bracelets and earrings. And it makes a great gift!

SHOPPING LIST

- 1 x 8 x 12" softwood*
- (1) 1½" finishing nail
- Copper ground wire, about 2' long
- 100-grit and 180-grit sandpaper
- Latex primer and paint

* This is a great project to use scraps from your scrap bin.

TOOLS

- Layout tools
- Tracing paper
- Scissors
- Cellophane tape
- Clamps
- Coping saw
- Hammer
- Drill with ¹⁄₁₆" and ⅛" bits
- Rasp
- Wood glue
- Paintbrush
- Wire cutters (sometimes called "snips")

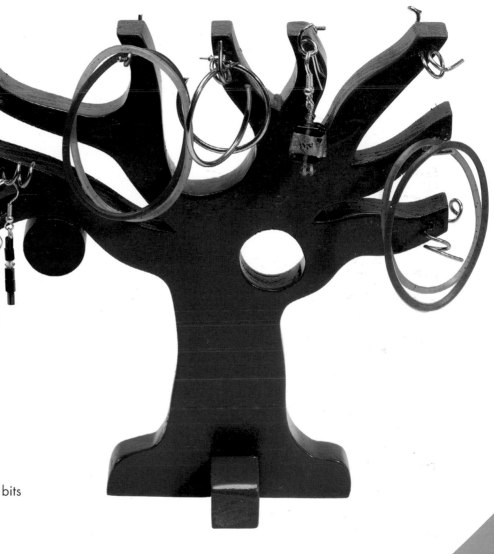

Jewelry Tree

CUT LIST

Code	Part	Number	Size	Material
A	Tree	1	¾" x 7¼" x 8"	Softwood
B	Base	1	¾" x ¾" x 4"	Softwood
C	Apple	1	(Cut from the knothole)	Softwood

Tracing the Patterns

1 Take a look at the pattern on page 98. It shows the three pieces you will cut out to build your Jewelry Tree. Note that the apple (C) is cut out of the tree (A) to make the knothole.

2 Using the tracing paper and a sharp pencil, carefully trace the outside edges of the tree (A) and the base (B). Also trace the knothole and the notch in the tree's trunk onto the tracing paper.

3 Carefully cut out the traced tree (A) and base (B) shapes with scissors.

4 Next, pierce the traced knothole shape with the tip of the scissors. Slip the scissors into the hole and cut out the knothole shape. (Don't worry about saving the small traced knothole you cut out.)

5 Finally, cut out the notch in the bottom of the tree (A) where the base (B) will be attached.

Cutting out the Tree

6 Lay the 1 x 8 board flat on your workbench. Place the traced tree (A) shape you cut out on the wood's face. The tree's flat base should be even with the squared end of the board. One side of the tree's shape should also be even with a side of the board. Align a long side of the base (B) with edge of your board as well. Lightly tape the tracing-paper patterns to the wood.

7 Now, transfer the patterns to the wood with your pencil. Be sure to also trace the details of the Jewelry Tree, including the outline of the base (B) and the knothole shape in the tree's trunk. Then pencil an X within the knothole near the cut line (you'll drill a hole here later).

8 Clamp your board to the workbench so that the tree's (A) traced limbs overhang the edge. Using your coping saw, carefully cut out the curving lines of the limbs. Take your time and adjust the clamped board as you work so you can saw the pieces neatly and easily. When you reach an inside point where two limbs meet, it's better to begin another cut from the outside than to try to turn the sharp corner with your saw's thin blade.

9 When you have sawed all the limbs, remove the clamped board, adjust and reclamp so that you can saw out the edges of the trunk. It's beginning to look like a tree!

10 Saw out the small notch in the base of the tree's (A) trunk. Make the notch as square as you can, reclamping the tree if necessary.

Removing the Knothole

11 Now for the knothole. Ask your adult assistant for some help with this step. Begin by making sure the tree (A) is clamped so that the knothole you traced overhangs the workbench's edge.

12 Chuck a 1/8-inch bit into your drill, and carefully bore a hole straight through the X you made in step 7.

13 To make the inside cut for the knothole, loosen the coping saw's tightening screw to remove the blade from the frame. Now, slide the blade through the hole you bored in step 12. Then reattach the blade to the frame.

14 Carefully saw out the circular knothole with your coping saw. Don't worry if your cutout isn't exactly round—knotholes aren't exactly round, either! You've also sawed out your apple (C) shape. Set the two pieces aside.

15 To complete your sawing, clamp the original board so that your tracing of the base (B) overhangs the edge of the workbench. Carefully saw out the base with your coping saw, and set the piece aside.

Adding the Wire Branches

16 You're nearing the finish line! Now it's time to lay out the holes for the wire "branches." Clamp the tree (A) onto the workbench so that the limbs overhang the edge.

17 Next, make an X about 1/4 inch from the end of each tree (A) limb and centered. The exact location isn't important, just do your best!

18 Ask your adult assistant for some help with this step. Chuck a 1/16-inch bit into your drill, and carefully bore a hole through each limb's X made in step 17.

Putting It Together

19 Assembling the Jewelry Tree is easy! First, you'll put the base (B) in the notch of the tree (A). Have your adult assistant hold the tree upside down (so it's resting on its branches). Set the base in the notch.

20 While your adult helper firmly holds the tree, gently hammer a nail through the center of the base (B) and into the bottom of the tree (A). Be very careful with this step—the branches of the tree are delicate and you don't want to smash them against the workbench.

21 Use your rasp to smooth out the apple (C). Make it nice and round.

22 Now you can attach the apple (C) to the tree (A). Stand the tree upright, resting it on the base (B). Put a drop of glue on the top of the apple and press it into the bottom of the lower left branch. Let the glue dry overnight.

Finishing Touches

23 Sand the Jewelry Tree. Use your rasp to smooth the knothole and other tight areas. Then use the sandpaper to smooth out the areas you rasped. Wipe off all the sawdust.

24 Prime and paint the Jewelry Tree. (You could paint the apple red, or any color you want.) Be careful when painting around the 1/16-inch holes in the branches. Don't let the paint fill up the holes.

25 Now you're ready to add the wire hangers. Cut the copper wire into 3-inch lengths with the wire cutters. Wrap each length of wire around the end of a pencil or small dowel to form a squiggle (like a pig's curly tail) or a hoop. Stick the end of the wire halfway through one of the holes you made in the branches. Make one hoop for each branch hole you drilled.

26 Well done! You've made a beautiful Jewelry Tree.

JEWELRY TREE PATTERN

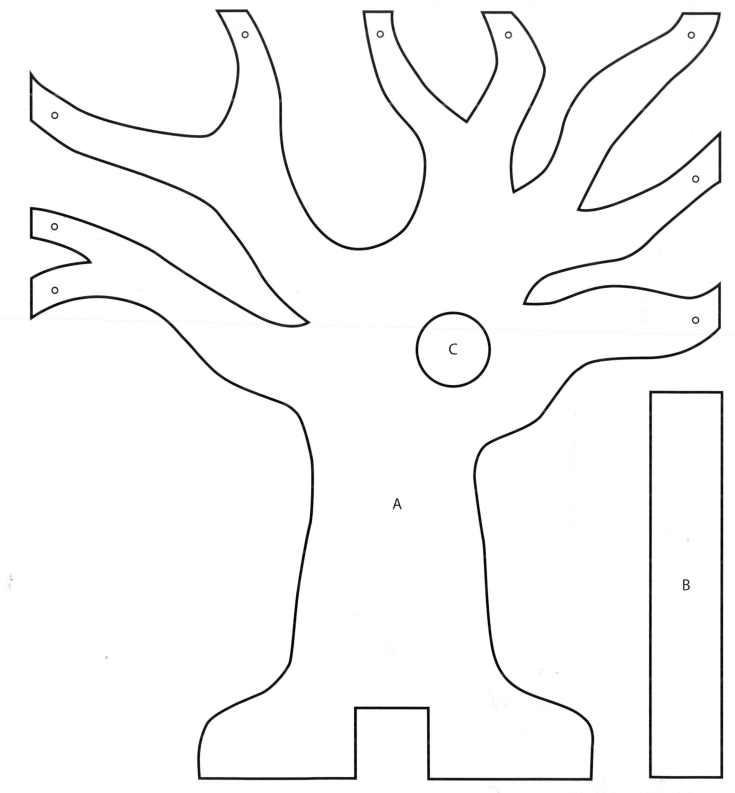

Desktop Organizer

Can't find your desk because of all the papers piled up everywhere?
This great-looking organizer will help you make some room to spread out.

SHOPPING LIST

- ¾" plywood, at least 12" x 30"
- ¼" plywood, at least 11" x 36"
- 1 x 2 x 3' softwood
- ¾" dowel, at least 6' total length
- 100-grit and 180-grit sandpaper
- Latex primer and paint
- No. 17 x ¾" brads
- No. 6 x 1⅝" screws

TOOLS

- Layout tools
- Handsaw
- Miter box
- Hammer
- Drill with ¾" and ⅛" bits
- Clamps
- Rasp
- 2" paintbrush
- Wood glue
- Screwdriver

CUT LIST

Code	Part	Number	Size	Material
A	Side	2	¾" x 12" x 12"	Plywood
B	Shelf	3	¼" x 11" x 11"	Plywood
C	Shelf back	3	¾" x 1½" x 11"	Softwood
D	Support dowel	6	¾" x 11¹¹⁄₁₆"	Dowel

Desktop Organizer

EXPLODED VIEW

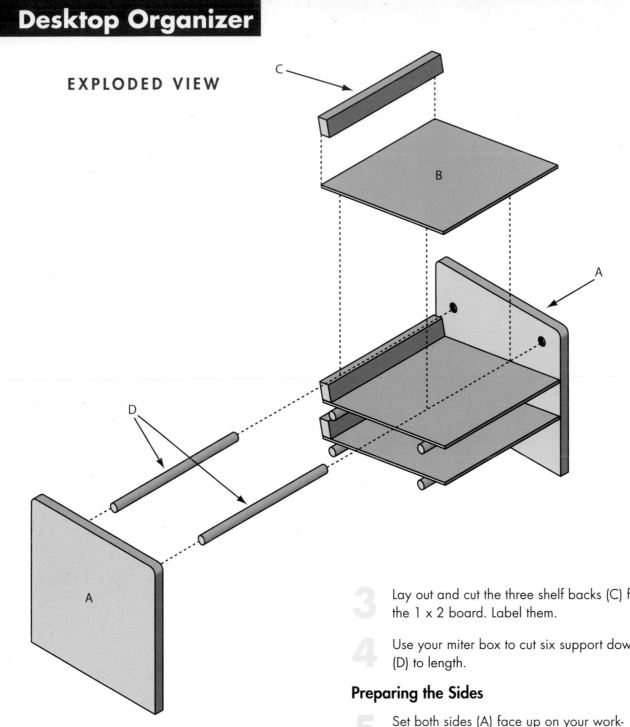

Cutting the Parts

1 Lay out and cut the sides (A) from the ¾-inch plywood. Label the pieces.

2 From the ¼-inch plywood, lay out, cut, and label the shelves (B).

3 Lay out and cut the three shelf backs (C) from the 1 x 2 board. Label them.

4 Use your miter box to cut six support dowels (D) to length.

Preparing the Sides

5 Set both sides (A) face up on your workbench. Mark the six pilot holes on the faces of each side as shown in Figure A. The support dowels (D) will fit in these holes. Notice that the layouts on the sides are reversed, like a pair of bookends.

6 Dimple the pilot-hole layouts on both sides (A).

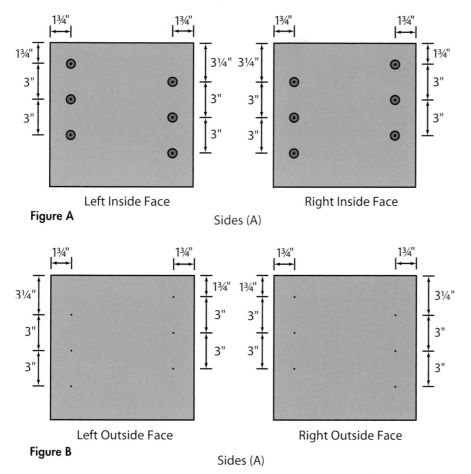

1¾" 1¾"   1¾"   1¾"

1¾"

3"   3¼" 3¼"

3"   3" 3"

3"   3" 3"

1¾"

3"

3"

Left Inside Face   Right Inside Face

Figure A   Sides (A)

1¾" 1¾"   1¾"   1¾"

3¼"   1¾" 1¾"

3"   3" 3"

3"   3" 3"

3"

3¼"

3"

3"

Left Outside Face   Right Outside Face

Figure B   Sides (A)

connects with the ¾-inch hole on the bottom face.

11 Repeat step 10 to bore pilot holes in the second side (A).

12 Finally, to make your organizer look its best, use your rasp to smooth and round each corner of both sides (A). Don't take off a lot; just enough so the corners are no longer square.

Sanding and Painting

13 It's easier to sand and paint this project before you assemble it. Sand all the parts well. Wipe off the sawdust and make sure everything is smooth.

14 Prime and paint all the pieces any colors you like.

7 Flag the ¾-inch bit to drill a hole ⅜ inch deep. Chuck the bit into your drill. Clamp the first side (A) to your workbench and drill through the holes as marked, stopping when the bottom of the flag touches the face of the wood.

8 Repeat step 7 to drill the holes on the other side (A).

9 Now you'll mark the smaller pilot holes on the opposite faces of both sides (A). These holes are for the screws you'll drive into the ends of the dowel supports (D). Flip the first side and transfer the layout marks shown in Figure B onto it. Do the same on the other side.

10 Dimple the pilot-hole layouts. Chuck the ⅛-inch bit into your drill. Carefully drill through each layout, making a ⅛-inch pilot hole that

Assembling the Shelves

15 First, you'll put the shelves (B) and shelf backs (C) together. Set the first shelf face up on your workbench. You'll attach a shelf back to the shelf face along the 11-inch edge (see Figure C). Run a thin line of glue along the edge of the first shelf back.

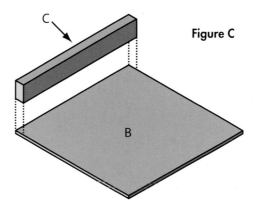

C

Figure C

B

16 Press the shelf back (C) onto the back edge of the shelf (B) to make an L shape.

17 Carefully flip the assembly so it rests on the shelf back (C). Hammer brads through the shelf (D) face and into the edge of the shelf back. Space the brads 2 inches apart.

18 Repeat steps 15 through 17 to attach the other two shelf backs (C) to the shelves (B).

Building the Sides

19 Next you'll join the sides (A) with the support dowels (D). Ask your adult helper to stand the first support dowel on end. Place the first side on top of it, fitting the end of the dowel into a ¾-inch hole.

20 While your adult helper holds everything together, drive a screw through the pilot hole in the outside of the side (A) and into the end of the support dowel (D).

21 Repeat steps 19 and 20 to attach the rest of the support dowels (D) to the side (A).

22 To attach the other side (A), flip the assembly so the side you just worked on is face down with the support dowels (D) standing up. Carefully set the second side's ¾-inch pilot holes onto the top ends of the dowels.

23 Drive a screw through each pilot hole as you did in step 20, but don't tighten the screws completely. You'll tighten them later, after the shelves (B) are in place.

24 Stand the sides (A) on end, the way the Desktop Organizer will sit on your desk. The higher support dowels (B) should be facing you. Slide the shelves between the sides so that they rest on the supports. The front edge of each shelf should be ½ inch behind the front edge of the sides.

25 Now fully tighten the screws in the second side (A). This will squeeze the shelves (B) between the sides, holding them firmly in place.

26 That's it! Put the Desktop Organizer on your desk and start sorting your papers.

Estimated Time: 4 to 6 hours

Study Partner

This desktop "study buddy" will make doing your homework a whole lot easier.

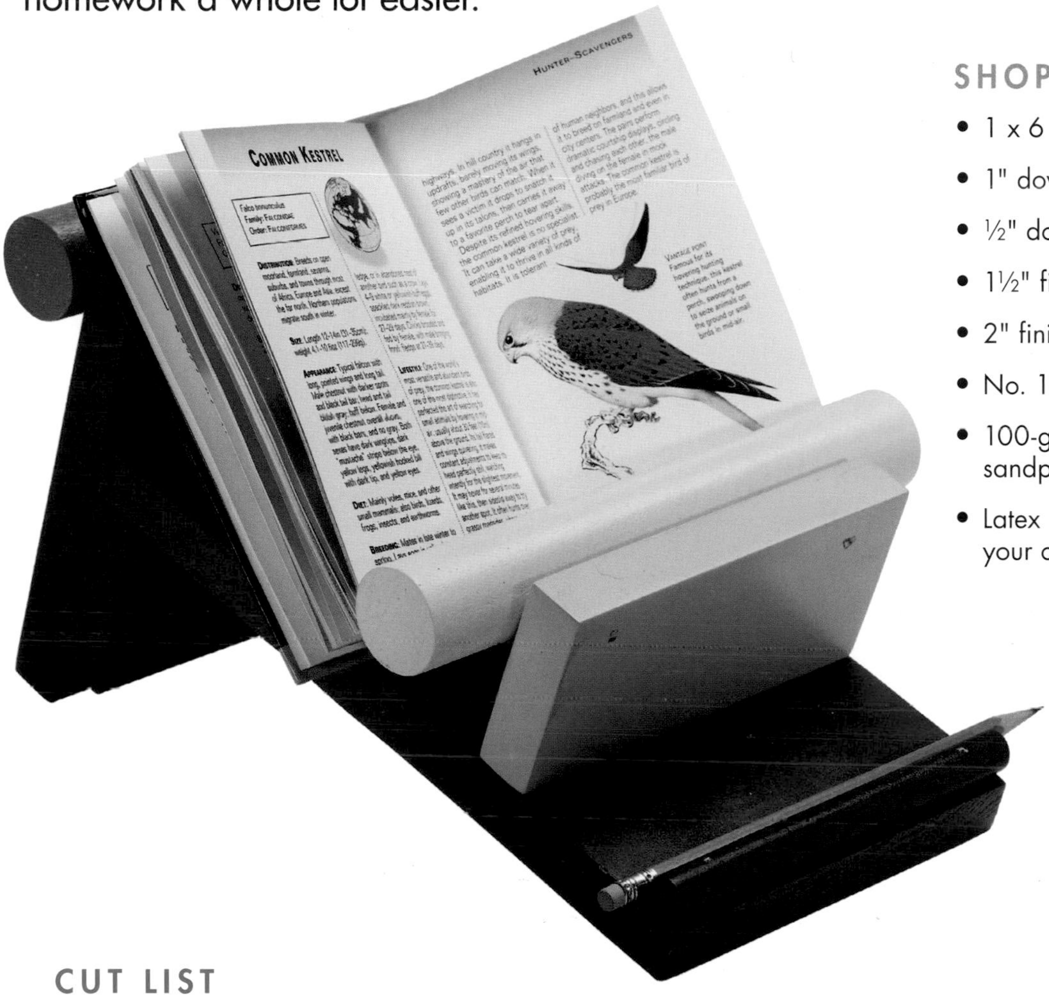

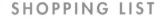

SHOPPING LIST

- 1 x 6 x 2' softwood
- 1" dowel, at least 18" long
- ½" dowel, at least 6" long
- 1½" finishing nails
- 2" finishing nails
- No. 17 x ⅞" brads
- 100-grit and 180-grit sandpaper
- Latex primer and paints in your choice of colors

TOOLS

- Layout tools
- Handsaw
- Miter box
- Hammer
- 1" paintbrush

CUT LIST

Code	Part	Number	Size	Material
A	Base	1	¾" x 5½" x 10"	Softwood
B	Top support	1	¾" x 5½" x 6"	Softwood
C	Bottom support	1	¾" x 5½" x 3"	Softwood
D	Brace	1	¾" x 5½" x 2½"	Softwood
E	Rest dowel	2	1" x 8"	Dowel
F	Pencil tray	1	½" x 5½"	Dowel

EXPLODED VIEW

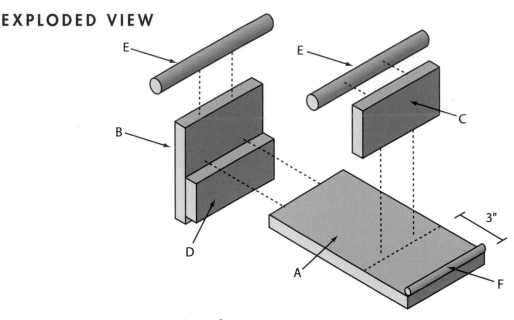

1 x 6 Board

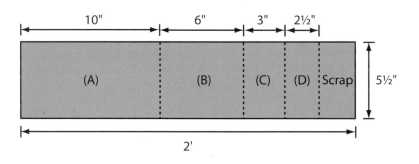

Cutting the Pieces

1 Lay out your Study Partner's base (A), top support (B), bottom support (C), and brace (D) as shown in the diagram of the 1 x 6 board above. Then cut the pieces to size and label them.

2 Now for the dowels. Lay out an 8-inch length of 1-inch dowel (E). Use your miter box and a handsaw to help you make the cut. Then label the piece. Repeat for the second 8-inch dowel.

3 Lay out a 5½-inch length of ½-inch dowel, saw it to length in your miter box, label it, and set it aside. This is your pencil tray (F).

Building the Top Support

4 You'll start by attaching the brace (D) to the top support (B). On the top support, measure and mark ½ inch from one end and use your square and a pencil to draw a line across the board where you've measured.

5 Set the top support (B) face up so that the line you drew is visible. Lay the brace (D) on the top support with the bottom end of the brace lined up with the mark ½ inch from the bottom of the top support. Make sure the side edges of both pieces are lined up. With your adult helper holding the two pieces together, hammer two 1½-inch nails through the brace and into the top support. Space the nails 2 inches apart.

6   Now you'll attach the first rest dowel (E) to the top support (B). Have your adult helper stand the top support on end, with the brace (D) near the bottom. Line up the rest dowel with the top end. While your adult helper holds everything in place, hammer two 2-inch nails through the rest and into the top support. Space the nails 2 inches apart. Set the top support aside.

Assembling the Base

7   Lay the bottom support (C) face up. Line up the second rest dowel (E) on the face of the bottom support, so it touches the end and edges (see Figure A). While your adult helper holds everything in place, hammer two 2-inch nails through the rest dowel and into the bottom support. Space the nails 2 inches apart.

Figure A

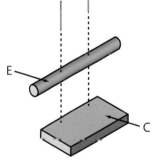

8   It's time to attach the bottom support (C) to the base (A). On the face of the base, measure and mark 3 inches from one end. Use your square and a pencil to draw a line across the board where you've marked.

9   Have your adult helper stand the bottom support (C) on its end (the one nearest the rest). With the rest (E) facing the longer side of the base (A), line up the top end of the bottom support with the line you drew on the face of the base. While your adult helper holds everything together, hammer two 1½-inch nails through the face of the base and

into the end of the bottom support. Space the nails 2 inches apart.

10   Now you'll attach the pencil tray (F) to the base (A) with the brads. Hold the pencil tray so it lines up with the bottom end of the base. While your adult helper holds everything in place, hammer two brads through the pencil tray and into the face of the base. Space the brads 2 inches apart.

11   Last step! Have your adult helper stand the base (A) on end (the end with the pencil tray attached to it). Rest the bottom face of the base against the brace (D) on the top support (B). While your adult helper holds everything together, hammer two 1½-inch nails through the top support and into the base.

Finishing Touches

12   Sand the Study Partner. Wipe off the sawdust.

13   Prime and paint the Study Partner. Let the paint dry for at least 24 hours.

14   Set the Study Partner on your desk. Now you can hit the books in style!

Estimated Time: 6 to 8 hours

Tabletop Easel

If drawing is another one of your hobbies, this adjustable drawing board is just for you!

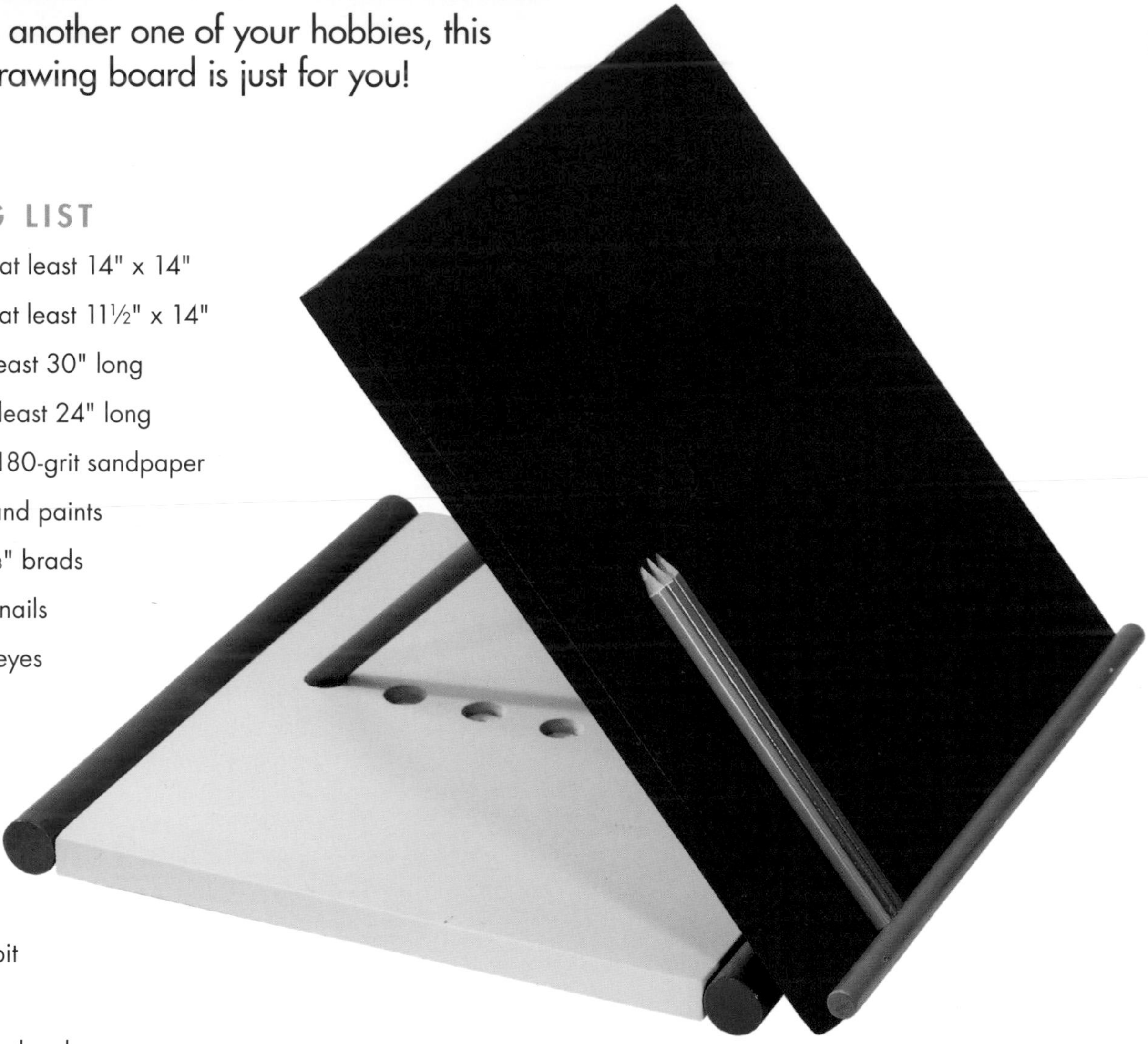

SHOPPING LIST

- ½" plywood, at least 14" x 14"
- ¾" plywood, at least 11½" x 14"
- 1" dowel, at least 30" long
- ½" dowel, at least 24" long
- 100-grit and 180-grit sandpaper
- Latex primer and paints
- 17 gauge x ⅞" brads
- 1½" finishing nails
- (6) ⅝" screw eyes

TOOLS

- Layout tools
- Handsaw
- Miter box
- Drill with ¾" bit
- Clamps
- 1" or 1½" paintbrush
- Screwdriver
- Needle-nose pliers

CUT LIST

Code	Part	Number	Size	Material
A	Backboard	1	½" x 14" x 14"	Plywood
B	Base	1	¾" x 11½" x 14"	Plywood
C	Base dowel	2	1" x 14"	Dowel
D	Tray dowel	1	½" x 14"	Dowel
E	Post	1	½" x 9"	Dowel

EXPLODED VIEW

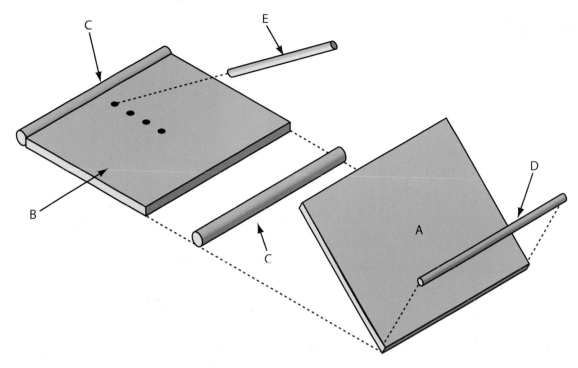

Cutting the Pieces

1 From the ½-inch plywood, lay out and cut the backboard (A) with your handsaw. Label the piece and set it aside.

2 Lay out, cut, and label the base (B) from the ¾-inch plywood. Set the piece aside.

3 Measuring from one end, lay out and cut both base dowels (C) from the 1-inch dowel using your miter box. Label the pieces and set them aside.

4 You'll cut two pieces from the ½-inch dowel. Lay out the length of the tray dowel (D) and use your miter box to make the cut. On what's left of the dowel, make another layout mark for the post (E). Again, use your miter box to make the cut. Label both pieces and set them aside.

Drilling Post Holes in the Base

5 Using Figure A as a guide, lay out the four ½-inch-deep holes on the base (B). Starting 1½ inches from one long edge, the holes run down the middle of the board. The hole centers are spaced 1½ inches apart.

Figure A

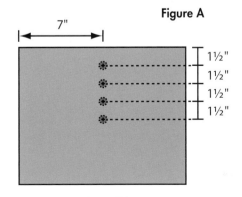

7"

1½"
1½"
1½"
1½"

Base (B)

6 Flag your ¾-inch drill bit for a ½-inch depth.

7 Clamp the base (B) to your workbench. Dimple the layout marks. Drill through them to the flagged depth of your drill bit, being careful to stop when the flag touches the wood's surface.

Painting the Parts

8 Sand all the parts. Wipe off the sawdust.

9 Prime and paint all the parts, using any colors you want.

TIP

> Whenever you paint the pieces of a project first, cover your workbench with cloth or cardboard before you start to build it. This will protect the paint from damage.

Attaching the Dowels

10 First, you'll attach the tray dowel (D) to the backboard (A). Because the tray dowel is so skinny and round, it's easier to put the brads into it first before you try to hammer the dowel to the backboard. Ask your adult assistant to hold onto one end of the tray dowel. Hammer the first brad through the center of the dowel's face. Stop when the tip of the brad starts to poke through.

11 Hammer two more brads into the tray dowel (D). Each of these brads should be 4 inches away from the brad in the center. Make sure the brads are in a straight line.

12 Place the tray dowel (D) on the face of the blackboard (A) so that it's lined up with the bottom edge. The ends of the tray dowel should be even with the sides of the backboard (see Figure B).

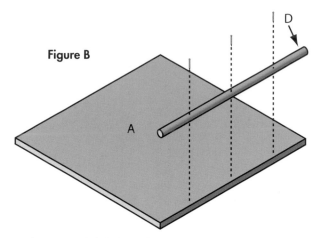

Figure B

With your adult helper firmly holding the pieces, hammer the brads through the tray dowel and into the backboard. Set this part of your easel aside.

13 Now you'll attach the base dowels (C) to the base (B) with finishing nails. Again, it's easiest to start the nails in the dowels before attaching the piece to the base. While your adult helper holds onto one end of the first base dowel, hammer a nail through the center of the dowel's face. Stop when the tip of the nail starts to poke through. Hammer two more nails into the base dowel. Each of these nails should be 4 inches away from the nail in the middle. Make sure the nails are in a straight line.

14 Repeat step 13, hammering three nails into the second base dowel (C).

15 Stand the base (B) on its 14-inch edge. Ask your adult helper to hold it steady. Center the base dowel (C) on the edge, with the tips of the nails aimed into the base. Make sure the ends of the dowel are lined up with the ends of the base (see Figure C). Hammer the nails through the base dowel and into the base.

16 Flip the base (B) so it rests on the base dowel (C) you just attached. Repeat step 15 to attach the second base dowel.

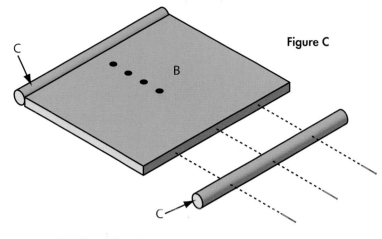

Figure C

Adding the Screw Eyes

17 The screw eyes will let you adjust the easel so you can put it in the perfect position. First, you'll attach the base (B) to the backboard (A) with four screw eyes.

18 Lay the side of the base (B) with the boreholes face-up. The front base dowel (C) should be facing you. (The boreholes are closer to the back of the base than the front.)

19 Make a mark 1 inch from the left end of the front base dowel (C). With your adult assistant holding the base (B) in place, put the first screw eye on the mark and gently tap the top with the hammer. This will drive the pointed end into the base dowel. Turn the screw eye clockwise with your fingers or with a screwdriver to drive it into the base dowel.

20 Repeat step 19 to drive the second screw eye into the front base dowel (C), 1 inch from the right side. Twist both screw eyes so that they are parallel with the ends of the dowel.

21 Now you'll attach two screw eyes to the back of the backboard (A). The eyes will hook into the eyes you just installed. Lay the backboard face-down so that it's resting on the tray dowel (D). Mark a point 1 inch from the bottom of the backboard and 1 inch from the left edge. Twist a screw eye into the mark.

22 Repeat step 21 to twist the second screw eye into the backboard (A), 1 inch from the right side. Twist both screw eyes so that they are parallel with the bottom edge of the backboard.

23 The post (E) attaches to the backboard (A) with a screw eye. Mark a point 9 inches from the bottom of the backboard and 7 inches from the left edge. Twist a screw eye into the mark.

24 Twist the last screw eye into the end of the post (E). Turn both screw eyes so that they are perpendicular to each other.

Attaching the Base to the Backboard

25 You're ready to attach the pieces of the easel. Join the screw eye in the post (E) to the screw eye in the middle of the backboard (A).

26 Look at the screw eye in the post (E). See the space between the metal eye and the screw? Grab that side of the eye with the needle-nose pliers. Hold the screw part with your other hand and bend the eye away from you just a bit. This will "open" the eye.

27 Repeat step 26 to open the screw eye in the center of the backboard (A).

28 Hook the two opened screw eyes together. Then bend the side of the eye back into place on each one with the needle-nose pliers so the eyes are "closed."

29 Repeat steps 26 through 28 to attach the screw eyes on the front base dowel (C) to the screw eyes on the back of the backboard (A).

30 Set the post (E) in one of the boreholes in the base (B). Put the easel on your desk and start your next masterpiece!

Estimated Time: 8 to 12 hours

Heart Box

A beautiful box for jewelry and keepsakes—with a secret compartment!

SHOPPING LIST

- ½" x 5½" x 18" oak craft lumber*
- ½" x 2½" x 24" oak craft lumber
- ¼" x 4" x 8" oak craft lumber
- 17 gauge x 1" brads
- ½" brass screw (for the false-bottom handle)
- (2) 1" x 1" brass butt-type hinges (with matching screws)
- (2) small plastic bumpers to protect the lid when it closes (ask for assistance to find this item)
- 100-grit and 180-grit sandpaper
- Sanding sealer
- Polyurethane
- Latex primer and red latex paint

TOOLS

- Layout tools
- Handsaw
- Clamps
- Tracing paper
- Coping saw
- Hammer
- Rasp
- Small screwdriver matched in size to your hinge screws
- 1" paintbrush
- Wood glue

*Oak craft wood is used for this project and listed as its actual size. Ask for ½-inch-thick and ¼-inch-thick craft wood at your lumberyard. For the false bottom piece, ¼-inch hardwood plywood will also work. If you can't locate craft wood, use standard ¾-inch-thick wood and ask your adult assistant to help you adjust the lengths of the pieces before you begin building.

EXPLODED VIEW

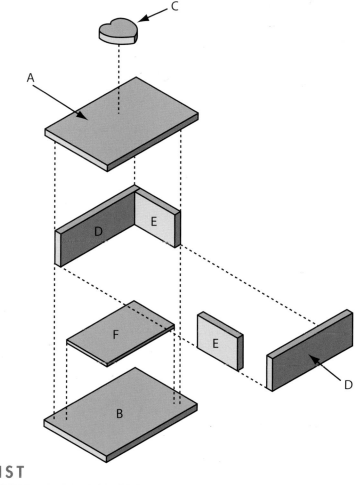

CUT LIST

Code	Part	Number	Size	Material
A	Lid	1	½" x 5½" x 8"	Oak craft lumber
B	Bottom	1	½" x 5½" x 8"	Oak craft lumber
C	Heart	1	½" x 3" x 3"	Oak craft lumber
D	Long side	2	½" x 2½" x 7"	Oak craft lumber
E	Short side	2	½" x 2½" x 3½"	Oak craft lumber
F	False bottom	1	¼" x 3⅜" x 5⅞"	Oak craft lumber or oak plywood

Cutting the Parts

1 Starting with the ½ x 5½-inch craft lumber, lay out, cut and label the lid (A) and bottom (B) pieces. Set them aside for now.

2 From the ½ x 2½-inch board, you'll lay out, clamp, and cut the two long sides (D) and the two short sides (E). Label the pieces and set them aside.

3 Now for the heart (C) that goes on top of the box. Trace the heart pattern on page 113 onto the top face of the remaining piece of ½ x 2½-inch craft lumber. The heart should be about 3 x 3 inches in size, but it doesn't have to be exact.

4 Clamp the board so the heart (C) shape hangs over the edge of the workbench. Cut out the shape with your coping saw.

5 Last cut! Set the ¼-inch-thick board flat on your workbench. Square the board if needed. Lay out the false bottom (F) on the square end. Clamp and cut out the piece. Label it and set it aside.

Assembling the Box

6 Ask your adult helper to stand one short side (E) on end. Set a long side (D) on top of it and align the ends to form an L shape. Hammer two brads through the face of the long side into the end of the short side. Space the brads about 1½ inches apart.

7 Repeat step 6 to attach the second long side (D) to the second short side (E).

8 Now you'll join together the two L-shaped pieces to make a box. Lay one short side (E) on its face, so the long side (D) is sticking up. Put the other L-shaped piece on top, lining up the corners. With your adult assistant holding the pieces together, hammer two brads (about 1½ inches apart) through the face of the long side and into the end of the short side.

9 Flip the box and repeat step 8 for the other box corner.

10 Now you'll attach the bottom (B) to the box. Set the box on its edges. Lay the bottom on top of the box. Adjust it so that it hangs over each side of the box equally (about ½ inch). With your adult helper holding the parts together, hammer brads through the bottom and into the edges of the box. To hit the edges of the box, hammer the brads about ¾ inch in from the edge of the bottom. Space the brads about 2 inches apart.

Making a Secret Compartment

11 Flip the box. Slide the false bottom (F) into it. Does it fit? Great! If not, use your rasp to remove some wood from the false bottom's edges until it does.

12 To make a handle for the false bottom (F), measure and mark its center. Drive a small screw about halfway into the mark you made. (If you want to be super secretive, don't put a handle on it.)

Putting a Lid on It

13 The last step is to attach the lid (A) to the box. Set the lid face-down. Measure and mark the space where the hinges will go—2 inches from either side along one edge. Line up the first hinge, with the hinge elbow and the other half of the hinge hanging over the edge. Drive a small screw into each hole in the hinge.

14 Repeat step 13 to attach the second hinge to the lid.

15 Rest the box on its bottom (B). Ask your adult helper to hold the lid (A) so the unattached halves of both hinges overlap the edge of one

of the long sides (D). Drive a screw partway through each hole in the hinge. Don't drive these screws all the way in yet!

16 Try closing the lid (A). If it closes neatly and fits squarely on the box, great! Drive the screws all the way in. If not, pull out the screws and adjust the position of the hinges until it does.

17 Add the two plastic bumpers to the underside of the lid, lining them up with the top front edge of the box so the wood parts are protected when the lid is closed.

Finishing Touches

18 Sand the jewelry box, the false bottom (F), and the heart (C). Use the rasp to smooth the corners of the heart. Wipe off all the sawdust.

19 Seal the jewelry box and false bottom (F) with sanding sealer. Let the sealer dry, and then lightly sand it with the 180-grit sandpaper.

20 Paint two light coats of polyurethane on the jewelry box and false bottom (F).

21 Prime the heart (C) and paint it red.

22 When the heart (C) is dry, run a few thin lines of glue on its backside. Press it to the center of the lid (A). Let the glue dry.

HEART PATTERN

Place-Card Holders

Having a party? Need seating arrangements? This project is a stylish way to show your friends where they'll be sitting at the table. Or use these holders to hold notes, photographs, lists, and more!

SHOPPING LIST

- ¾" thick softwood scraps, at least 3½" wide
- 100-grit and 180-grit sandpaper
- Latex primer and paints in your choice of colors
- Construction paper or thin card stock (optional)

TOOLS

- Tracing paper
- Cellophane tape
- Scissors
- Layout tools
- Clamps
- Coping saw
- 1" paintbrush

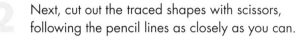

Tracing the Patterns

1 Begin by using your tracing paper and a sharp pencil to trace the patterns on page 116. So the paper won't shift around, tape the tracing paper lightly to the page before you make your tracings.

2 Next, cut out the traced shapes with scissors, following the pencil lines as closely as you can.

3 Lay your ¾-inch scrap of softwood flat on your workbench. Place one of the traced shapes on top of the wood's face so that the base (or bottom) of the shape lines up with a square edge of the wood.

4 Holding the tracing lightly in place with your fingers, transfer the outline of the shape onto the wood.

5 Now, place a second tracing on another area of wood at least one inch from your first penciled outline. Repeat steps 3 and 4. (Allowing a little room between outlines will let you saw out the pieces more easily). Continue tracing the shapes until you have six different penciled outlines.

Cutting out the Shapes

6 Clamp your board to the workbench with one of the penciled outlines hanging over the edge.

7 Carefully saw out the shape with your coping saw. Take your time and adjust the clamped board as you work. When you reach the inside of a sharp turn (or "inside corner") on your traced outline, it's better to begin another cut from the outside than to try to turn the sharp corner. When your first piece is sawed out, set it aside.

8 Continue clamping and sawing until you have all six shapes cut out.

Cutting the Paper Slots

9 The slots in the top of each shape will hold the paper place cards. Clamp one of your cut-out shapes with the top edge of the shape overhanging the workbench edge just a little.

10 Use your coping saw to make a simple, shallow cut about ½ inch deep into the top of the shape.

11 Repeat steps 9 and 10 for each shape.

Finishing Touches

12 Sand all the place-card holders. To sand the slots, fold a piece of sandpaper in half, so that the gritty side faces out. Run the paper back and forth through the slot. Wipe off all the sawdust.

13 Prime and paint the place-card holders.

14 Cut place cards out of construction paper or thin card stock. Write your friends' names on them, place them in the slots, and put the holders where you want your friends to sit.

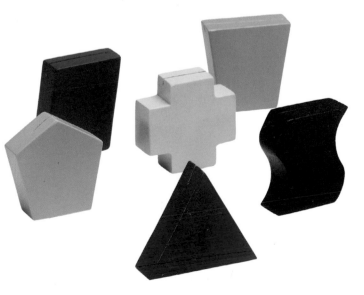

PLACE-CARD HOLDER PATTERNS

Key Condo

Are your parents constantly searching for their keys? Make this project for them and add a couple pictures of yourself so they're reminded of who gave them such a helpful gift.

SHOPPING LIST

- 1 x 6 x 24" softwood*
- ⅜" softwood dowel, at least 18" long
- 100-grit and 180-grit sandpaper
- Latex primer and paints in your choice of colors
- (2) photographs of your family, friends, or pets, sized to fit in the two cutout openings of the project.

* You can also use ½" craft lumber to make cutting with the coping saw easier.

TOOLS

- Layout tools
- Handsaw
- Clamps
- Coping saw
- Hammer
- Drill with ⅜" bit
- Miter box
- Wood glue
- 1" paintbrush
- Cellophane tape

CUT LIST

Code	Part	Number	Size	Material
A	Condo	1	¾" x 5½" x 17¼"	Softwood
B	Peg	7	⅜" x 2"	Dowel

EXPLODED VIEW

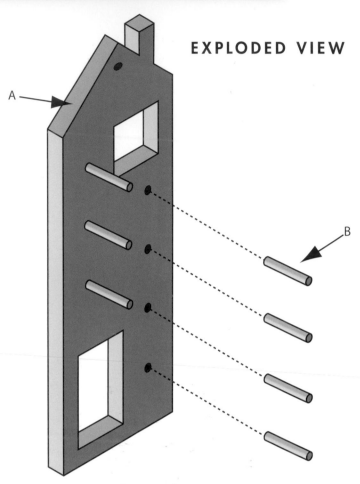

A

B

Laying out the Condo

1 Lay out and cut the condo (A) piece with your handsaw to its 17¼-inch length. Make sure the ends are square.

2 Look carefully at Figure A, which shows the layout for the condo (A). Note the roof and chimney layouts, the two cutouts for the window and door, and the pilot-hole layouts for the seven pegs.

3 Using Figure A as your guide, carefully lay out all the lines and pilot-hole marks.

4 Clamp the board securely to your workbench with the condo's (A) roof and chimney layouts overhanging the edge.

5 Use your coping saw to cut each line of the roof and chimney. Saw slowly and steadily— there's no rush!

Cutting out the Doors and Windows

6 With a ⅜-inch bit chucked in your drill, carefully bore one hole in any inside corner of the window and door layouts. This gives you an access hole for your coping saw's blade.

7 Remove the blade from your coping saw. Slip the blade through one of the holes you bored, and tighten the blade back onto your saw.

8 Now, saw out the layout's shape. Adjust the clamped condo (A) as needed to make sawing easier. When you reach a corner of the layout, back up your blade slightly, and saw toward the next

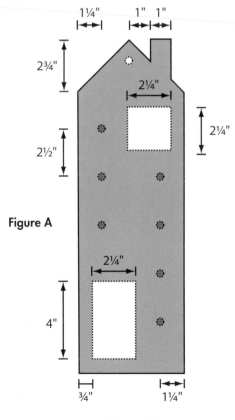

Figure A

Condo (A)

line instead of trying to turn the corner sharply. When the first cutout drops out of the layout lines, you can neaten up any rough corners with your coping saw.

Cutting the Pegs

9 To make the pegs (B), use your pencil and tape measure to lay out a mark 2 inches from one end of the dowel. Then make more marks at 4 inches, 6 inches, and so on until you've made seven marks.

10 Use your miter box to cut the pegs (B) to size. Take your time and saw the small dowels with very light pressure to avoid splintering the wood.

Making the Peg Holes

11 Set your condo (A) flat on the workbench and dimple the peg layouts for each pilot hole. Flag the ⅜-inch bit for a ¼-inch depth.

12 Chuck the bit into your drill. With your adult helper holding the condo securely, drill the holes at the peg layouts, stopping as the bottom of the bit's flag touches the top of the wood.

13 Dimple the hanger-hole layout at the top of the condo (A). Remove the flag from the drill bit—you'll be boring right through the board.

14 With your adult assistant holding the condo (A) securely, drill the hole.

Attaching the Pegs

15 Set the condo (A) face-up. Put a drop of glue on the end of a peg (B). Set the peg in a borehole. Tap the top of the peg gently with the hammer to get it in place. With a damp cloth, wipe up any glue that squeezes out.

16 Tilt the peg (B) slightly toward the top of the roof. This angle will keep the keys from slipping off!

17 Repeat steps 15 and 16 to put all the pegs (B) in place. Let the glue dry.

Finishing Touches

18 Sand all the parts. Prime and paint all the pieces. It's easiest to paint the condo (A) piece first, and then paint all the pegs (B).

19 Tape or glue photos behind the window and door cutouts.

20 Mount the Key Condo on the wall, using the pilot hole at the top. Then hang up those keys!

Round and Round Media Tower

Fill this multilevel storage unit with your favorite CDs and DVDs. Then just give it a spin to grab what you want.

SHOPPING LIST

- 1 x 10 softwood, at least 3' long
- 2 x 4 softwood, at least 4" long
- 1 x 4 x 6' softwood
- 1" x 20" softwood dowel
- 1½" finishing nails
- No. 8 x 2" screws
- 100-grit and 180-grit sandpaper
- Latex primer and paints

TOOLS

- Layout tools
- Handsaw
- Miter box
- Clamps
- Hammer
- Drill with 1¼" and ⅛" bits
- Wood glue
- Screwdriver
- Rasp
- 1" paintbrush

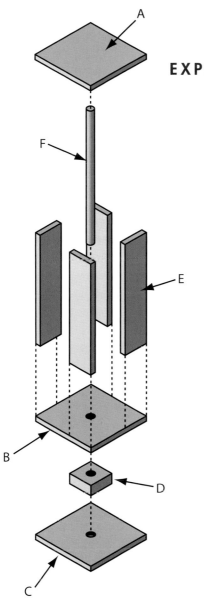

EXPLODED VIEW

CUT LIST

Code	Part	Number	Size	Material
A	Top	1	¾" x 9¼" x 9¼"	Softwood
B	Bottom	1	¾" x 9¼" x 9¼"	Softwood
C	Base	1	¾" x 9¼" x 9¼"	Softwood
D	Collar	1	1½" x 3½" x 3½"	Softwood
E	Side	4	¾" x 3½" x 16"	Softwood
F	Center post	1	1" x 19½"	Dowel

Cutting All the Parts

1   Using the diagram of the 1 x 10 board as your guide, lay out and cut the top (A), bottom (B), and base (C). Label the pieces and set them aside.

2   Lay out and cut the collar (D) to length from the 2 x 4. Label the piece and set it aside.

3   Now for the sides (E). Lay out and cut the four sides from the 1 x 4. Label the pieces and set them aside.

4   Lay out the center post (F). Use your miter box and handsaw to cut the dowel to length. Label it and set it aside.

1 x 10 Board

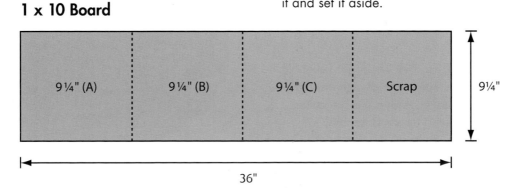

Estimated Time: 8 to 12 hours

Travel Checkers

Want a go-anywhere game? This checkers set comes with pieces that won't fly all over the car.

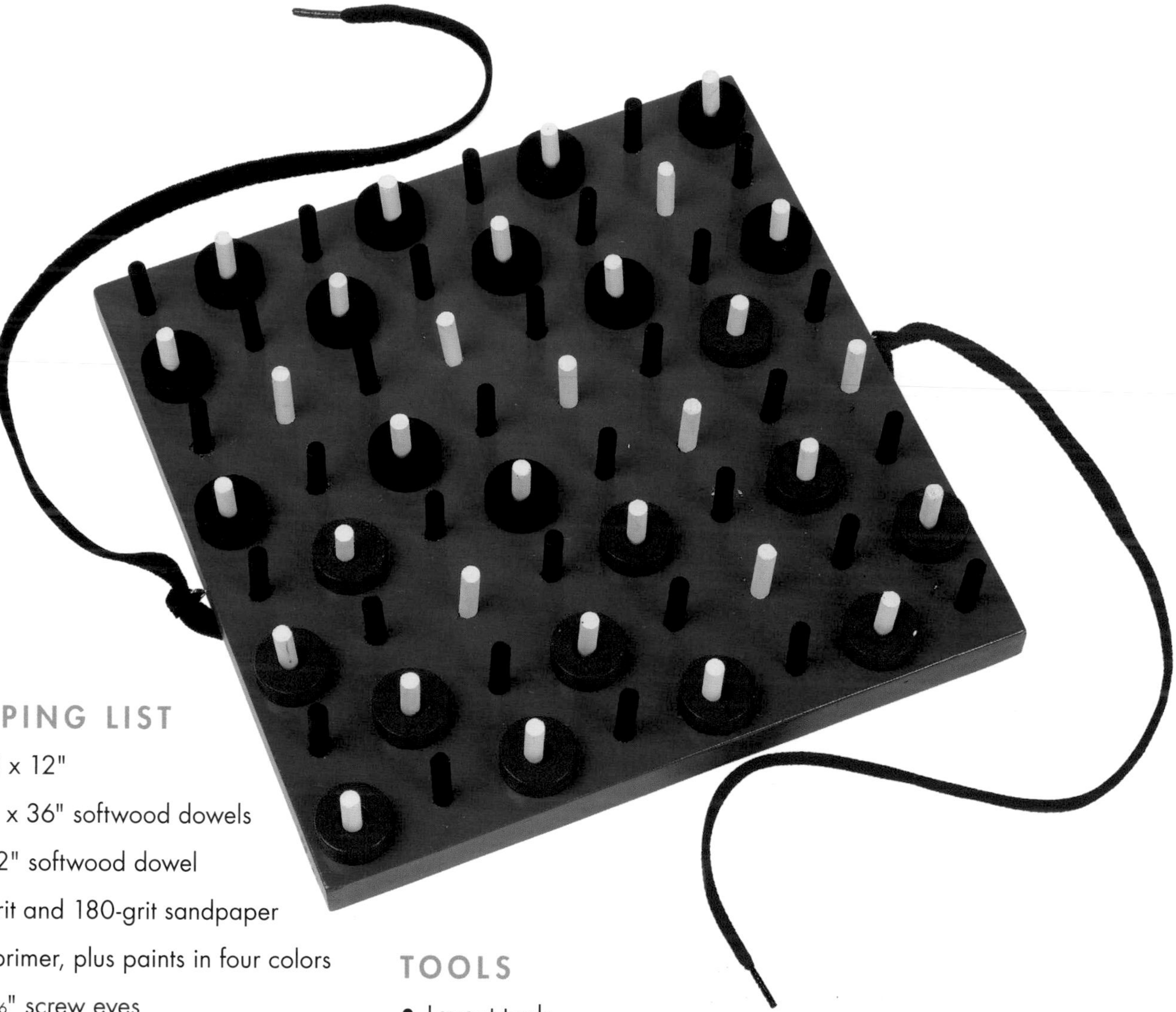

SHOPPING LIST

- 1 x 12 x 12"
- (3) ¼" x 36" softwood dowels
- 1" x 12" softwood dowel
- 100-grit and 180-grit sandpaper
- Latex primer, plus paints in four colors
- (2) 1¹⁄₁₆" screw eyes
- (2) shoelaces, each at least 14" long

TOOLS

- Layout tools
- Handsaw
- Clamps
- Hammer
- Drill with ¼" bit
- Miter box
- Slip-joint pliers
- Wood glue
- 1" paintbrush

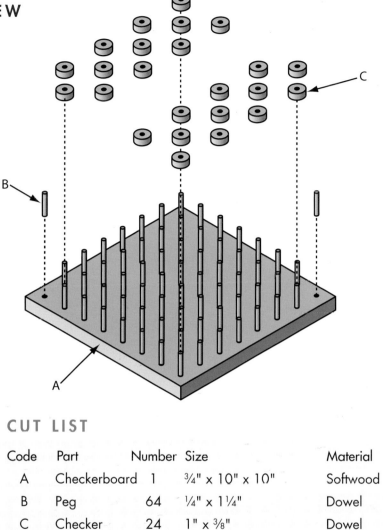

CUT LIST

Code	Part	Number	Size	Material
A	Checkerboard	1	¾" x 10" x 10"	Softwood
B	Peg	64	¼" x 1¼"	Dowel
C	Checker	24	1" x ⅜"	Dowel

Building the Board

1 Lay out the checkerboard (A) from the 1 x 12 board. If you use a square corner of your lumber as the starting point for your layout, you'll only need to make two cuts. Start with the rip cut along the grain of the board. Then make the crosscut. You should now have a square. Label the piece.

2 It's time to transfer the layout marks you see in Figure A to the face of the checkerboard (A).

Begin at one corner and lay out a spot every 1¼ inches along the side. (There should be seven marks.) Repeat for the other three sides.

3 Now connect the marks you made with straight lines. You'll draw 14 lines, dividing the checkerboard (A) into 64 squares.

4 The last layout step is to draw two diagonal lines across each of the small squares, connecting the corners to form an X.

1.   2.   3.   4.

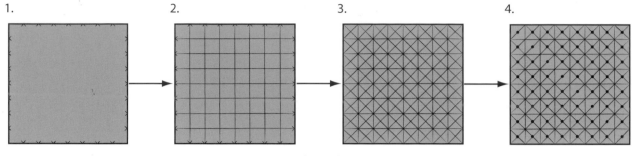

Figure A

5 The center of the X mark on each square is where you'll drill a hole for a peg (B). First, place scrap wood between the checkerboard (A) and the workbench. Then clamp the pieces together. Dimple the center of each square. Flag the ¼-inch bit to bore a ⅜-inch-deep hole. Chuck the bit into your drill and drill each hole. Stop drilling when the bottom of the flag touches the surface of the checkerboard. (If your arm gets tired, ask your adult assistant to drill.)

6 When all of the holes are drilled, set the checkerboard (A) aside.

Cutting the Pegs

7 Grab two of the ¼-inch dowels. Beginning at one end, measure and mark a line every 1¼ inches. Then, on the third ¼-inch dowel, measure and mark nine more 1¼-inch lengths. (You won't need to use the whole dowel.)

8 Cut the pegs (B) from the dowels. Be sure to use the miter box. Take your time and use light pressure while sawing: this will help prevent the wood from splintering. No need to label these pieces. That would take forever! Just count them to make sure you have 64. Now would be a good time to take a break!

Making the Checkers

9 Lay out twenty-four ⅜-inch lengths on the 1-inch dowel. Then use the miter box to make

the cuts. Don't label these pieces. Just count them to make sure you have 24 checkers (C).

10 Next you'll drill holes in the pieces you cut in the previous step. Grab a checker (C) and mark the center, which should be ½ inch from the edge. Mark the center again, from the other edge, so your marks intersect in the center. Do this for each checker.

11 Place scrap wood between a checker (C) and the workbench. Have your adult assistant hold both pieces of wood in place using the slip-joint pliers. Dimple the center mark. With the ¼-inch bit chucked into your drill, carefully bore all the way through the center mark. Repeat this step for each checker (C).

Setting up the Board

12 Assembling the checkerboard (C) is easy. All you have to do is glue the pegs (B) into the board. Lay the checkerboard face up, with the boreholes facing you.

13 Put a drop of glue on the end of the first peg (B). Set it in a borehole. If the peg doesn't go into place easily, use the hammer to tap lightly on the end. Adjust the peg so it's straight. Wipe up any glue that squeezed out.

14 Repeat step 13 to put the rest of the pegs (B) in the checkerboard (A). Allow time for the glue to dry.

Finishing Touches

15 Sand the checkerboard (A) and all the checkers (C). Wipe off all the sawdust.

16 Prime and paint the checkerboard, starting with the board (A) and then the pegs (B). Paint the pegs two different colors in diagonal rows. (See the photo on page 124.)

17 Prime and paint the checkers (C). Make 12 pieces one color and the 12 other pieces a different color.

Storing Your Checkers

18 Attach a screw eye to opposite ends of the board. Ask your adult assistant to stand the checkerboard (A) on end. Make a mark in the center of the edge, 5 inches from each end. Put the first screw eye on the mark and gently tap the top with the hammer. This will drive the pointy end into the edge. Turn the screw eye clockwise with your fingers to drive it in.

19 Flip the checkerboard (A) and balance it carefully on the screw eye you just attached. Repeat step 18 to drive the second screw eye into the opposite end of the board.

20 Knot an end of one shoelace around a screw eye. Thread one color of checkers onto the shoelace. Tie the other end of the lace around the same screw eye.

21 Repeat step 20 to attach the second shoelace to the checkerboard. Now your checkers won't get lost when you're not playing. Challenge someone to a game!

HOW DO I PLAY CHECKERS?

Your checkers game is played only on the white pegs shown in the photo on page 124. Set one color of checkers on the 12 white pegs closest to one end of the board and the other 12 checkers on the 12 white pegs closest to the opposite end of the board. Decide who moves first.

A piece may move forward one square at a time, diagonally. If one of your checkers is next to one of your opponent's checkers—and the next diagonal square beyond it isn't occupied—you can jump over your opponent's checker and remove their piece from the board. If, after you jump, there's another opponent's piece next to yours with a free space behind it, you may jump it as well. Keep jumping until you can no longer jump.

When one of your checkers reaches an empty peg at the opponent's end of the board, it becomes a "king" checker. ("King" your piece by adding another checker of your color on top of it). Your king checker may now move and jump diagonally both forward and backward, which really gets the game going!

The winner either captures all of the opponent's checkers or forces the opponent into a position where none of her checkers can move in any direction. If this were chess, you could yell out "Checkmate!" Instead, be sure to thank your opponent for a good game.

Estimated Time: 3 to 4 hours

High Flyer

When this lightweight plane isn't soaring through the air, it can decorate your room.

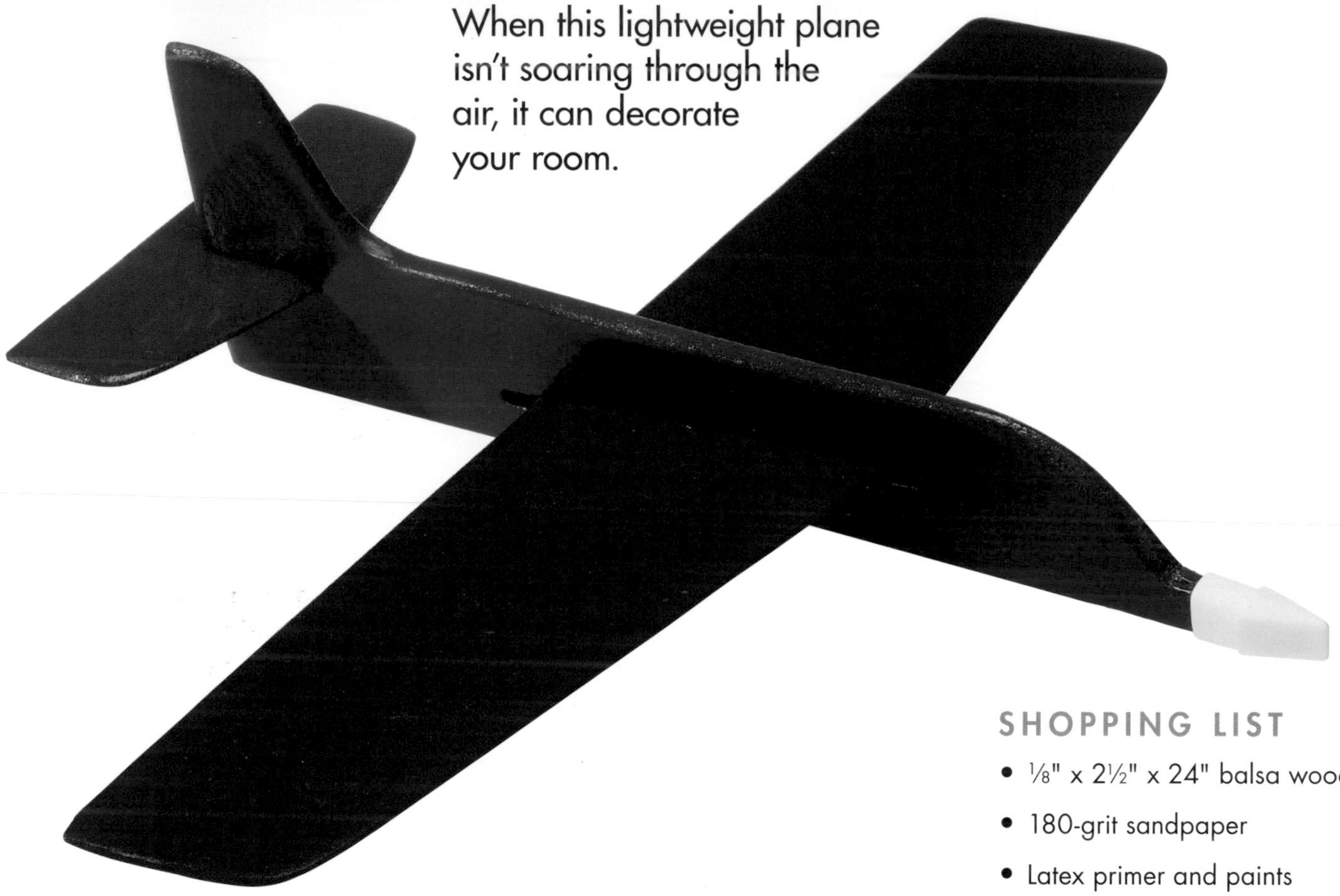

SHOPPING LIST

- ⅛" x 2½" x 24" balsa wood
- 180-grit sandpaper
- Latex primer and paints
- Rubber eraser tip for a pencil
- Pushpins (optional)

TOOLS

- Layout tools
- Photocopier
- Box cutter
- 1" paintbrush
- Wood glue (optional)

CUT LIST

Code	Part	Number	Size	Material
A	Body	1	¼" x 3½" x 9"	Balsa wood
B	Wing	1	⅛" x 3½" x 12"	Balsa wood
C	Tail	1	⅛" x 1⅝" x 4"	Balsa wood

EXPLODED VIEW

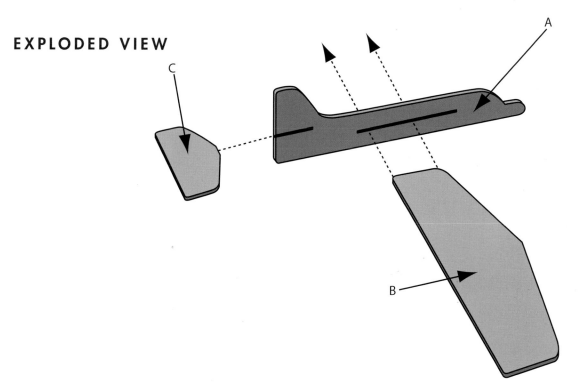

Cutting out the Parts

1 Use a photocopier to enlarge the patterns on page 131 by 25%. Cut out both patterns and trace them onto the balsa wood. Be sure to trace the two slots inside the body (A).

2 Ask your adult assistant to help you use the box cutter to cut along all the lines you've drawn (except for the slot lines). To use the box cutter, hold it in the hand you write with. Gently press the tip of the blade into the balsa wood. Carefully pull it along the line. Make several short, shallow cuts to pierce the wood rather than one deep cut. Label the pieces A, B, and C.

3 Place the body (A) atop a large piece of scrap wood. Have your adult assistant help you with this step: use the box cutter and an edge of your square to cut out the slots. Be sure to use a light, steady pressure on the box cutter. (You don't want to make the slots larger than necessary or you won't have a snug fit when you attach the wings and tail to the airplane.)

4 Test fit the pieces. Slip the wing (B) into the middle slot of the body (A). It should be snug, but not tight. If the fit is too tight, the body may split. Go back to step 3 to widen the slot.

5 Test the fit of the tail (C) in the slot at the end of the body (A). If it's too tight, return to step 3 to widen the slot.

Sanding and Painting

6 It's easiest to sand and finish the pieces before assembling the flyer. Lightly sand the outside edges with 180-grit sandpaper and dust them off. Because the balsa wood is so fragile, don't use 100-grit sandpaper. Prime and paint the parts.

Building the Plane

7 To put your balsa flyer together, slip the rubber eraser tip over the nose of the body (A).

8 Carefully slide the wing (B) into the slot in the middle of the body (A). Center the wing.

9 Slide the tail (C) into the slot at the end of the body (A). Center it, just as you did with the wings. Now you're ready for a test flight!

Taking to the Skies

10 For your first test flight, choose a windless day or somewhere protected from the wind. Holding the base of the body just behind the wings between your thumb and forefinger, throw the flyer gently into the air. Watch how it flies. You can adjust the flight by moving the wings.

11 If the flyer stalls (floats nose up but doesn't go forward), slide the wing toward the tail. Try it again.

12 If the flyer takes a nosedive, slide the wing toward the nose.

13 To make distance flights, add a pair of pushpins to the nose of the flyer. This will give the flyer a little more weight. Slip the ends of the pins into the eraser tip on the nose, one on each side. Try it again.

14 Did your flyer crash-land and break or split? You can glue the pieces back together as long as the break or split goes with the grain of the wood. Let the glue dry before taking the High Flyer out for another flight. If the break is across the grain, make a new piece.

HIGH FLYER PATTERNS

(Enlarge by 25%)

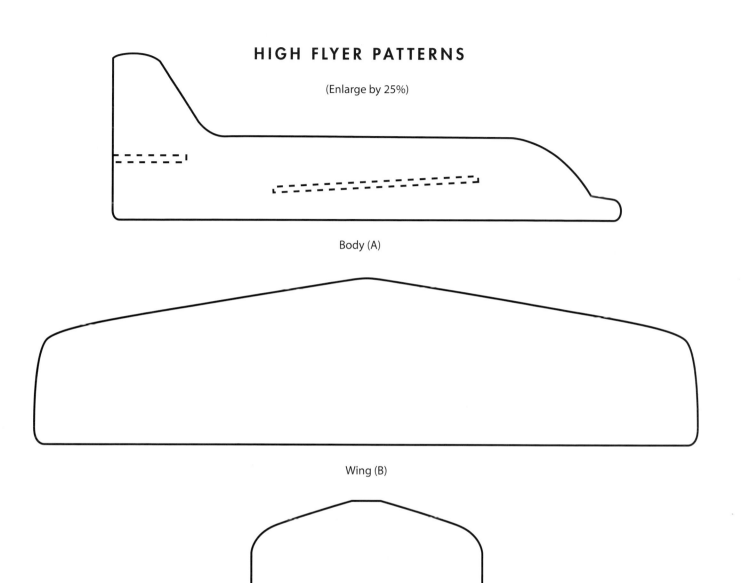

Body (A)

Wing (B)

Tail (C)

Six Birds Tessellation Puzzle

Put your coping saw skills to the test with this puzzle project and explore the amazing world of tessellations—repeating shapes that fit tightly together.

TOOLS

- Tracing paper
- Layout tools
- Cellophane tape
- Scissors
- Clamps
- Coping saw
- Rasp
- ½" or 1" paintbrush

SHOPPING LIST

- ¼" x 16" x 16" birch plywood or craft lumber
- 100-grit and 180-grit sandpaper
- Latex primer and paints

Tracing the Pieces

1 Use your tracing paper and a sharp pencil to trace the pattern on page 140. Lightly tape the tracing paper to the page before you make your tracing so the paper won't shift around.

2 Next, cut out the traced shape with scissors, being careful to follow the pencil lines exactly.

3 Lay your wood face up on your workbench. Place the traced shape on top of the wood's face. Transfer the outline of the shape onto the wood with your pencil.

4 Move the tracing to another area of wood at least 1 inch from your penciled outline and repeat step 3, transferring another outline. (Allowing a little room between outlines will let you saw out the pieces more easily). Continue tracing until you have six penciled outlines.

Cutting out the Pieces

5 Clamp your board to the workbench with one of the penciled outlines hanging over the edge.

6 Carefully saw out the shape with your coping saw, making a special effort to keep the blade straight up and down. Follow the line as much as possible. Take your time and adjust the clamped plywood as you work. Remember that when you reach the inside of a sharp turn (or "inside corner") on your traced outline—such as where the bird's wing meets the body—it's better to begin another cut from the outside than to try to turn the sharp corner. When your first piece is sawed out, set it aside.

7 Continue clamping and sawing until you have all six puzzle pieces.

Putting It Together

8 Put the tessellation puzzle together. Do the pieces fit? Great! If not, sand the edges that don't fit. Use your rasp or sandpaper. If a piece absolutely won't fit, set it aside and trace another. Cut it out and try it again.

Finishing Touches

9 Sand each piece of the tessellation puzzle. Wipe off the sawdust.

10 Prime and paint each piece. You can try painting them different colors.

11 Add details if you want—eyes, beaks, tail feathers, etc. Use either your smallest detail brush or a felt-tipped pen.

12 Show the puzzle to your friends and see if they can put it together. Then come up with your own shape to make another puzzle!

BIRD TESSELLATION PATTERN

Glossary

Balsa wood. A lightweight, easily breakable lumber.

Chucking. Inserting a bit into a drill.

Coping saw. A C-shaped saw used to cut curves or make inside cuts.

Craft lumber. Small, sanded pieces of lumber.

Crosscutting. Cutting straight lines across the grain.

Dowel. Lumber shaped into a round pole.

Edge. A narrow side that runs the length of a board.

End. A short edge of a piece of lumber. The ends are the two edges that are farthest apart.

Face. One of a board's two wide, flat surfaces.

Face joint. A face joint is made of two boards fastened face to face.

Fence. A guide that keeps the wood at the same distance from the saw.

Finish. Paint, varnish, or stain put on wood to change its appearance and protect it by sealing out dirt and dampness.

Grain. The thin, wavy lines in wood that run along the faces and edges of the board. Grain shows the direction the tree grew.

Grit, sandpaper. The size of the particles on sandpaper. Grit gets smaller in size as the grit number increases, so 100-grit is rougher and removes more wood than 180-grit.

Handsaw. A saw with a handle at one end that you pull back and forth across a piece of wood to make a cut.

Hardwood. Heavy, durable wood that can be more expensive and difficult to work with than other woods but has a pretty grain.

Joint. Places where pieces are fastened together.

Kerf. The groove that a saw makes when you pull it back and forth across wood.

Knot. The place where a tree's limb entered the trunk of the tree.

Lattice. Thin strips of lumber.

Layout tools. Tools for making and marking measurements—a tape measure, a pencil, and a square.

Nominal size. The names used to sort, name, and sell lumber. Nominal size is a name only—the wood actually measures a slightly different size.

Parallel. Two objects that are an equal distance apart at every point.

Perpendicular. Forming a right angle.

Pilot hole. A hole drilled before putting in a screw to keep it from splitting the wood.

Plywood. Wood slices glued together to form a flat sheet that is inexpensive yet very strong.

Primer. A coating spread on wood to seal it. Primer can be used to make the wood grain show up or to create a surface for paint to stick to.

Radius. The measurement from the center to the outside edge of a circle.

Rasp. A tool that scrapes off little bits of wood as you push the blade forward.

Right-angle joint. Two boards fastened together at a 90-degree angle. A box is made with four right-angle joints.

Ripping. Cutting in the same direction as the grain of the wood.

Ryoba saw. A kind of handsaw that cuts as you pull it toward you.

Semigloss. A slightly shiny kind of paint, also called "satin."

Softwood. Wood that is light-colored, lightweight, fairly strong, and easy to hammer a nail into, but doesn't have a grain as pretty as hardwood.

Square. An L-shaped device with a blade marked with measurements. To check square is to use the square tool to determine if a piece of lumber is placed straight with right angles.

Stain. A finish that changes wood's color while letting the grain show through.

Standard lumber. The most commonly used boards, sorted by type, grade, and size.

Varnish. A shiny, clear finish that seals dirt and dampness out of wood.

Waste side. The wood on the side of the cut line that will be cut off and not a part of the final project.

ACKNOWLEDGMENTS

To Anne Kelley McGuire for her project suggestions and support.

And to the staff at Lark Books for artful guidance and enthusiasm in the building of this book.

METRICS

Need to convert measurements in this book to metrics? Here's how:

To convert inches to centimeters, multiply by 2.5.

To convert feet to meters, multiply by 0.305.